Waiting
in the Wings

Other books by the author:

Heroes and Saints & Other Plays
The Last Generation
Giving Up the Ghost
Loving in the War Years: Lo que nunca pasó pos sus labios
Cuentos: Stories by Latinas (co-editor)
*This Bridge Called My Back: Writings by Radical Women
  of Color* (co-editor)

Waiting in the Wings

portrait
of a
queer
motherhood

Cherríe Moraga

Firebrand
Books

Ithaca, New York

Earlier versions of several selections from this work have been published in *Living Chicana Theory* (Third Woman Press) and *The Politics of Motherhood: Activist Voices from Left to Right* (University Press of New England).

Book and cover design by Debra Engstrom
Cover photographs of the author by Patrick "Pato" Hebert

Printed in Canada

10 9 8 7 6 5 4 3 2 1

Library of Congress Cataloging-in-Publication Data

Moraga, Cherríe.
    Waiting in the wings : portrait of a queer motherhood / by Cherríe Moraga.
    p.   cm.
    ISBN 1-56341-093-1 (cloth : acid-free paper). — ISBN 1-56341-092-3 (pbk. : acid-free paper)
    1. Motherhood. 2. Lesbian mothers. 3. Pregnancy in middle age. 4. Artificial insemination, Human. 5. Mexican American women—Sexual behavior. 6. Hispanic American lesbians. 7. Middle aged lesbians. I. Title
    HQ759.M8617   1997
    306.874'3'086643—dc21
                                            97-37241
                                             CIP

To that hole in my heart,
Rafael Angel Moraga—
thank you for staying.

And, gratefully, to the nurses at San Francisco Kaiser ICN, 1993

Contents

On Naming, Genre, and Language

Many of the names throughout this essay have been changed to respect the privacy of certain individuals and to acknowledge that this writing is my own personal "fiction." In the case of the "character" of my lover-partner, I refer to her here as "Ella," the Spanish word for *she*, where the double *ll* is pronounced as *y*. Throughout the text, I do not distinguish Spanish from English with a different typeface. This more closely reflects the fluid bilinguality of the Chicana/o voice. My closest friends are referred to as "comadres," a Mexican term denoting an intimacy similar to that of a family member.

I have at times reconfigured the chronology of events depicted in *Waiting In The Wings* in favor of the requirements of dramatic storytelling.

We do not know where death awaits us:
so let us wait for it everywhere.
To practice death is to practice freedom.
A man who has learned how to die
has unlearned how to be a slave.

Michel de Montaigne

Prologue: The Long Hard Path

It's like making familia from scratch
each time all over again...
with strangers, if I must.
If I must, I will.

Cherríe Moraga, *Giving Up the Ghost*

Lesbians don't make babies with our lovers.

We make babies with strangers in one-night stands or on the doctor's insemination table, with friends in a friendly fuck or a loveless mason jar, with enemies who at the time were husbands or boyfriends, or with ex-husbands whom our children call papi and whom we may still consider family. We cannot make babies with one another. Our blood doesn't mix into the creation of a third entity with an equal split of DNA. Sure, we can co-adopt, we can co-parent, we can be comadres, but blood mami and papi we ain't.

I know the stories that we only admit to one another in private, our children's hunger for "normalcy," no matter how much they love us. A brilliant butch woman told me years ago about a boy she had raised with his mother for many years. One night her heart broke when, tucking in the bespectacled boy of ten, he wrapped his arms around her neck and called her daddy, with everything he had in him. When I finally met the boy, I saw that he shared María's poor eyesight, wit, and brainy humor. Most of all, he learned how to be a boy from María. He learned masculinity from María and she was a wonderful male role model: the best of fathers with a woman's compassion.

I have been the lesbian lover of a mother. I know what it is to live in that uncertain role as the "nonbiological parent," such a cold anglo-american term.* But at least in the beginning, and perhaps on a deeper level, I asked the same of my partner, Ella. I asked her not to be a mother, but only a lover of my child, a lover to me. Probably hers is the most noble of gestures, certainly more noble than offering sperm and having the privilege of knowing your bone-memory lives on in another being, without duty.

---

*I am speaking here of the relationship between the blood mother, her child, and her partner. When a lesbian adopts or co-adopts a child with her partner, parental rights in relation to the child may be interpreted quite differently.

In the beginning, I didn't know how much mother Ella would be to our child. Neither did she. I didn't know how much I wanted to share motherhood. I didn't know how soft and hard it is—that letting go—to entrust another human being in the raising of your child. I have, at times, rigorously protected my "single motherhood" for fear of losing my son to *anyone*. Still, I would not have embarked on this journey alone: I chose motherhood because I knew Ella was that quality of woman who would never just up and leave.

"I'm going to do this," I told her. "Will you go there with me?" Had Ella answered no, quite possibly I would have gone no further.

I imagine most people would think it radical to take it upon one's lesbian self to make such a proposal first to her partner, and then to a gay man, a generation younger. *I'm going to do this. Will you help me?* Without question in another era, in another geographical region outside of San Francisco, another cultural point of reference, my having a baby as an avowed lesbian would have been a radical phenomenon indeed. And in most circles I imagine it still is. But not in my own circle, not in the circle where I have constructed familia, not with a woman partner as firm as the steady changing earth, not amongst the women I call comadres, the donor I now call compadre, nor among my blood familia. Having Rafael Angel was the most natural evolution of two lives—his and my own—the most logical next step on a road whose mysterious twists and turns make me marvel daily.

I tell friends that I almost missed Rafaelito. That he had been there, waiting in the wings, and I could hear his voice in the most remote corners of my dreams and in the raising of other women's children. That is how I account for his precipitous birth at only twenty-eight weeks of gestation. He was a spirit who, for some time, was wanting to get here, through me. And when I finally opened my heart and listened, he took hold of me right away. I was pregnant with the first insemination; six months later he was born, weighing only two pounds six ounces.

One of my most beloved friends said to me upon the news of

my pregnancy, "La admiro, you're doing it your own way." Now sixty, Myrtha had raised three sons almost single-handedly. What was there to admire in me? But I understood what she meant. I had come to my motherhood along the long hard path. Nothing has been a given for me, not even my womanhood.

I was blessed to be born into a huge extended Mexican family. A family in which aunts and uncles acted as surrogate parents, and cousins were counted among siblings, and where my grandmother, Dolores, who died at the age of ninety-six, presided matriarchal y mandona over the lives of some one hundred-plus relatives. Today, the living Moraga clan spans five generations and a full century of U.S.-born mestizos, residing in what was once the Mexican territory of Alta California.

My parents, now in their seventies and eighties, live in the same house that I have known since the age of nine. My sense of home was formed both inside the walls of that 1920s stuccoed two-and-a-half-bedroom suburban Los Angeles structure as much as it has been shaped outside of it. When I return to visit, I sleep in the same room (now "the tv room") where my sister and I, as teenagers in the 1960s, shared apocalyptic nightmares and dreams of sexual awakening. (Although I knew, even then, that the shape of her dreams was very different from my own.)

Growing up, the *we* of my life was always defined by blood relations. *We* meant family. We were my mother's children, my abuela's grandchildren, my tíos' nieces and nephews. To this day, most of my cousins still hold onto a similar understanding of *we*. Not I. In 1975, at the age of twenty-two, I came out as a lesbian and named as female the subject of that earlier adolescent sexual dream life. Once out, although I did not keep my sexuality secret from the closest members of my family, I knew it could never be fully expressed there. So, the search for a *we* that could embrace all the parts of myself took me far beyond the confines of heterosexual family ties. I soon found myself spinning outside the orbit of that familial embrace, separated by thousands of miles of geography and experience. Still, the need for familia, the knowledge of familia, the capacity to create familia remained and has always informed my relationships and my work as an artist, cultural activist, and teacher.

I've always experienced my lesbianism as radically different from most white gays and lesbians. For that reason, I have never been a strong proponent of lesbian marriages (although I've officiated at a few), nor particularly passionate about the domestic partnership campaigns for which my white middle-class gay counterparts continue to rigorously fight. No, I've always longed for something else in my relationships—something woman-centered, something cross-generational, something extended, something sensual, something humilde ante la creadora. In short, something Mexican and familial but without all the cultural constraints.

Rosie hunches over the pages of her notebook, blocking her tight-fisted scrawl with the draping sleeve of her flannel shirt. She is my student. At fifteen, Rosie has more piercings etched into her flesh than her number of years on the planet. She puts down her pen and looks up at me with wide eyes. "Am I doomed," she asks with those eyes. I know her family story—the brutal fact of abuse, the white rapist father, the silent latina mother. So she cuts at her body and drives ink and all matter of rings into her skin. She sticks liquid needles into her veins and wonders if she'll survive the season. The season of being young and queer and on the street because home is a more dangerous place to be. She is my daughter.*

I want something more than 12-step for Rosie and her Latina lesbian kind. She deserves more than Christianity or goddess worship, more than politically correct lines that take away our edges, our outrage, our pasión. She deserves familia resurrected and repaired, by *us*.

*For five years I directed a writing-for-performance theater troupe called the DramaDIVAS, of which "Rosie" was a member.

My search for this familia has been played out (sometimes with a vengeance) with every lover I have had, regardless of age or race or cultural background. With each one, I thought myself committed "for the duration," for surely we were at war, trying to make a place for lesbian love in a woman-hating world. And as I tried to "save" each one of my lovers, and all her children (those incarnate and those invisible), the invisible wreaked havoc on our loving: the rapes, the incest, the battering, the betrayals, the alcoholism, the orphanhood. We try to repair—as we repeat the scenarios—the familial lessons learned, for better or worse, about loving.

There was a time for me when my sense of family, and by extension *community*, was strictly women, then strictly lesbian, then strictly women of color, then strictly Chicana/o, then strictly Latina lesbian. But these categories of identity could never fully encompass the people in whom I placed my trust. In each of those worlds I found abrazo y rechazo, and I soon learned to make alliance within that less-defined area and more reliable project of *common cause.*

What is sex or prayer (I don't know which) is the spring's sunlight descending into the cooling goldenrod hills. I watch it retreat, starting my bath in the evening light, finishing in darkness. I watch my womb grow, watch the sudden transformation of my body like some holy miracle. I try to reach somewhere wounded and orphaned inside of me and bring this sudden image of my queer womanhood into view: I, the object of my own desirous, lesbian, woman-hungry eyes. I, a mama, too, like all the mamas I have longed for and loved.

As a child and a tomboy, I never fantasized about having kids. No more than most little boys do, dreaming about a brood of five sons—enough to make up a basketball team. When I came out as a lesbian at the age of twenty-two, I simply assumed that since I would never be married to a man, I would never have children. So while my sister was busily making babies every three or four years, I was busily making lovers (yes, about every three or four years). Then, at the age of thirty, it hit me: I was a woman and, therefore, potentially *capable* of having children.

This may sound strange, a statement of the blatantly obvious, but buried deep inside me, regardless of the empirical evidence to the contrary, I had maintained the rigid conviction that lesbians (that is, those of us on the more masculine side of the spectrum) weren't really women. We were women-lovers, a kind of third sex, and most definitely not men. Having babies was something "real" women did–not butches, not girls who knew they were queer since grade school. We were the *defenders* of women and children, children we could never fully call our own.

I had lived out that fantasy in many ways. In my mid-thirties, I was involved with a wonderful artist and her young child, whom I will call Joel. In the three years of my relationship with his mother, I had grown to think of Joel–whether sanctioned or not–as my own. Then one day, I lost them both without warning and with great wrenching. Not so much from the woman, but from the child. This was the baby I had watched become a boy, whom I had walked to kindergarten, taught how to ride a two-wheeler and build sand castles on the beach. We had hiked in the foothills together, I pointing out leaf and flor. I had explained the meaning of morning frost to him, the metamorphosis of polliwogs to frogs, of caterpillar to marvelous mariposa. And I had also made his morning breakfast, bathed him in the evening, picked him up from daycare, and given him medicine in the middle of the night. I didn't do these things equally with his mother, but I was a partner to her and a parent to him to the degree I was allowed. Simply, I knew Joel with a kind of heart's knowledge that I have never been able to completely erase.

I remember once, just before the "official" breakup, Joel and I had been separated from his mother and each other for many weeks. He had been staying with his father, and after much urging from me, the man let me have Joel overnight. The first thing I did was give Joel a much-needed bath. Pulling him out of the tub I wrapped him in a huge cotton towel and took to grooming him, tenderly cleaning his ears with a Q-tip, clipping his finger- and toenails, rubbing his smooth cafecito skin with sweet oil. Suddenly, he looked up at me and blurted out, "You're my mom." We were both missing her badly. And at that moment I could already taste their forever-absence from my life.

The only and final time I was allowed to see Joel after a six-month separation, he became very angry and refused to hold my hand in our last hour together. At the time, I didn't understand. We had gone on an overnight camping trip and had built a toy-sized grave for his abuelo, who had recently passed. We constructed the cross out of tiny twigs. I had felt so close to Joel then, making up our own ceremony for a man who had eaten at my table and yet whose death I learned of thirdhand. Joel's sudden anger as he left hurt me, but later I realized maybe it was too painful for him, too—these long absences and strained reunions. During the six-hour trip back to San Francisco, I barely missed what could have been a fatal car accident. I cursed my car and raged against my predicament, my lack of bona fide motherhood *or* fatherhood, and the absolute impotence of being the lesbian lover of a mother. *Men (and women) come and go,* I could hear my mother's refrain. *All you really got are your children.*

But Mamá, I lost the child, too.

The dreams where Joel appears, always in crisis, have gradually dissipated with the birth of my son, Rafael Angel. Still I think of him often. Kindly, sadly. I remember one incident when I was putting Rafael back into his carseat after shopping, and I called him Joel. It shocked me, for although I had almost called Rafaelito that name many times before, I usually caught the word before it slipped into the air, never to be retrieved. I felt guilty, I wasn't sure why, and I assured my son, *tú eres el único, hijo,* the way we must reassure our lovers when we, by accident, call them by a past lover's name. When this happens between lovers, we are mortified. *What does it mean?* We fear that she—the other beloved—was the greater love. And sometimes she was. But sometimes she was merely a profound touching, an awakening that will always be remembered by that name, even when the same place is touched by another. That is who Joel is to me, my first (almost) son. And the mother he called forth in me made my hunger for Rafael Angel all the more urgent: *a child that would never be taken from me, a child to raise from scratch.*

One thing Joel's presence in my life taught me was that, without realizing it, I had grown up to be woman enough, on my own terms, to mother a child. The child grew inside me, the loss of the child, the discovery of mother, the recognition that I had nursed dozens of hungry women throughout my life as I had my own mother, from the time I could remember, and in that resided my lesbian conviction, my lesbian loving. I am a daughter and have always loved the daughters in all our beauty and brokenness. *But what of children?* Not until 1992, a handful of years after the loss of Joel, could I answer that question unequivocally and affirmatively: I wanted a child. I was forty years old.

The pages that follow are my own queer story of pregnancy, birth, and the first years of mothering. It is a story of one small human being's—my son's—struggle for survival/for life in the age of death/the age of AIDS. Much of the writing here was first composed as journal entries. Later, I returned to those passages to fill in the details of events which, at the time, I was too immersed in living to describe.* In retrospect, this book is a kind of poet's memoir, for even giving birth does not satisfy the artist's hunger to create. Finally, this is the story of faithfulness between two lesbian lovers/ mothers and the family that has sustained us.

San Francisco, 1996

*Original journal entries are italicized.

I
City of the Angels

An angel came to me last night
sat   patient   in the fog
of my night sweats...

His tears washed away
my lesions
said he wanted me
to...heal the earth...

Leave my mark
with my halting steps...

He wanted me
to fly.

Tede Matthews, "Angel Wings"

The feast of the epiphany, a good day to start a life.

When Ella and Pablo sat around me on my bed after the insemination, a comforter covering me, my legs propped up in the air with pillows, I felt "made love to." That's the expression that came to mind, and that was the feeling exactly. The way I always imagined becoming pregnant would feel like, in the best of scenarios. But the insemination had nothing to do with sex or orgasm or excitement, except our three-way titillated embarrassment over the procedure. Pablo stood in the bathroom, trying to think about anything sexier than the mouth of a mason jar, while Ella and I waited nervously in the bedroom together, Ella practicing pumping water in and out of the syringe. Still, for all its awkwardness, I can say that the experience was probably the best loving I'd ever known. I am still awed by the fact that these two people loved me enough to go through whatever embarrassment to help me conceive.

"That's all there was to it?" Ella's mom would ask us months later.

"Yes."

"But it's so simple."

"Yeah," I answer, "one way or another that sperm has just gotta get inside you."

Very simple...and unromantic. Yet I did feel made love to. And whether pregnant or not, I knew I would never forget what that softness felt like, my legs up and open to receive whatever destiny had decided for me. I close my eyes and dream Pablo as a sweet twin lover. I put my mouth and nose into the hollow of Ella's neck, breathe her in and I am sustained. Momentarily, there is tranquilidad.

28 enero/Los Angeles

Today I feel my hormones acting up, blowing me up, sitting heavy on my chest. I wonder if this is all just a bad case of PMS. I wonder if I am pregnant. I feel my body a stranger. I am without desire. What happened to desire? Or is it that my desire is so great and lies muted somewhere inside me.

I wish I knew how to pray. I clasp together my hands before my altar, light a vela, study la virgen's impassive expression, wave the scent and heat of copal over all my openings and long for una respuesta...a word, an image, a vision. Does the journeying I must make right now involve miles of physical territory, or is it an interior map I need to explore through reading, reflection, conversation? I proceed with the plan of having a baby because I have only myself, the kindness of friends, the cosmos to trust. I experience pain often in my womb and vagina. I don't understand the signs. I ignore them, yet I know that having this baby requires listening to my body, requires diet, exercise, counsel, prayer, apoyo, hogar, fuerza y paciencia.

I am on the verge of tears in this writing. I keep getting flashbacks, mental glimpses of my parents waiting for me at the Hollywood/ Burbank airport. With each visit, they seem a bit smaller physically, a bit older, slightly more vulnerable. Standing at the gate, they greet me with expectant, anxious eyes, my dad always noticing me a few seconds after my mom. I am filled with emotion. This family means so much to me, this family slipping away. I grow to comprehend, somewhere in my heart, how transitory this physical life is.

I miss L.A. In a way I miss how I am essentially L.A. born and bred, but my spirit resides elsewhere.

29 enero

Returning from the play reading in Los Angeles, I ignore what is most evident—my desire for this child. I give it half-hearted attention, not being able to fully believe it could happen to me. In the deepest places I am afraid of the commitment, I am afraid of the disappointment. I am afraid to want this baby and be unable to have it. My sister and Ella both try to convince me to take a home pregnancy test, but I am superstitious. I think if I want it too bad, it won't happen.

Finally, coming back from L.A. I promise Ella that if she buys the test, I'll take it. She does. In seconds after I put the required few drops of urine onto the test paper, two pink lines appear indicating I'm pregnant. There is no ambivalence in those lines: they are a dark, solid, unwavering pink, and there are clearly two of them. Ella and I look at each other, dumbfounded. I still can't believe it. How could two tiny lines, such insignificant markings, pronounce something as irrevocable as a human life? Ella can't believe my resistance. She volunteers to take the test. If hers turns up with only one line, then will I be convinced? Yes, I promise. Sure enough, one line and a faint one at that. We stare at each other in the bathroom, looking back and forth at her test and mine...her test and mine. Ella's eyes are dancing with excitement, but I can't fully take it in and make a silent agreement not to count on any babies until I get a blood test from the doctor. It isn't denial, exactly, more like this is too good to be true.

30 enero

It is nearly February, and I realize that in weeks I am to take off to Guatemala for the Popol Vuh Project. But I have made no plans and I grow tired at the thought of it. I don't know why, but I think of staying home. Reading all I can on the Popol Vuh, beginning to work*

---

*During the time of this writing I was working on *Heart of the Earth*, a play adaptation of the Popol Vuh, the Quiché Maya creation myth and heroes story. *The Hungry Woman: A Mexican Medea* is a play based on the Greek tragedy and the Mexican myth of La Llorona.

on Medea, slowing down. I think of visiting la partera, Angelina, seeking her consejo about this maybe-baby, improving my diet, my exercising. For some reason, I want to take care of myself.

3 febrero

Just got a call from the doctor. Bona fide pregnant. First try.

I haven't written of my days with the reproductive sciences, the fertility experts, the sonograms of my fetus-sized fibroids—all benign and thoroughly unproductive. I had all the tests months ago, in advance, to make sure everything was in working order "down there"—the tubes clear, the hormones balanced—in short, a healthy habitat. The fertility specialist had given me the odds: bad even for forty-year-old heterosexuals who are "doing it all the time," he said. Still, I'd give it a shot. How? He wanted to know but didn't ask. Weeks later, when I came in with the news of my pregnancy, whispering to the nurses, "It was homemade," they all cracked up, teasing the doc. So much for science. He took it in good stride, even came to see my baby, months later in the ICN, telling me he had never seen me look so happy.

15 febrero

I dream two images of my baby. One where he is born already a grown boy, like my student Pedro, then older like Pablo. So beautiful, so sensual. I touch him all over. I can't believe he is mine, although I am disappointed that he was born a boy. I touch his penis inside his pants. I know I have gone too far, but I am delighting so much in his beauty. Then my baby is born again. This time a tiny beautiful dark-haired Mexican girl. I am in heaven. I remember looking at the baby girl's genitalia, thinking at first the swollen round vagina is balls, then realizing, no, it is a vagina. The joy is endless, although through-out both parts of the dream I wonder how it is my baby was born so fast when she was just nothing more than a seed inside of me. She is transparent. Her skin a see-through casing holding in muscle and bone. I know in the dream that the skin will take on the appearance of flesh later.

19 febrero

This baby settles into me. If I were to write about being a writer, I would say it has something to do with the contemplative life, the life of standing at the end of a pier, the sun an hour into the horizon of black bay waters. The skyscraper reflections make me believe that at forty my life is barely beginning. I know it is this life I carry within me that causes me to imagine a future, a future I could never dream in any lover, only in blood-familia, only in my sister with whom I shared a bedroom and a dream-life for twenty years. As girls we believed we would never be parted. Not really.

I stare into the black sea and know my eyes mirror that same endless dark depth. I float out under the Golden Gate Bridge and into the Pacific, knowing with complete clarity that my life will take me (us) to many lands, to many languages. How is it that travel seems more possible now, thinking of this life...this barely formed being? I walk back to my car at a brisk pace. Driving home, the radio announces the Senate passage of a bill outlawing the entrance of HIV-infected immigrants. One reporter speaks of 270 Haitians imprisoned in camps, "a living hell," he calls it. And a prayer rises up to my lips. "We all deserve a future."

I return home to cook catfish. Full of gratitude, the barriers between Ella and me dissolve. And I believe we will never be parted. Not really.

28 febrero

It is barely past midnight when I awaken, trembling from the nightmare. I only remember Ella's face, like my sister's, and her bottomless rage. My entire body fills with the fire of fear first, then despair. I do everything in my power to calm her down. It is too late, all I can do is escape the dream. I will myself awake. My body bounds with adrenaline. I feel the new life inside me stir. And I think of how this small smudge of life knows me like no other, how once I knew my mother the same way and was born with the knowledge of her torment. This is not the legacy I wish to pass onto my baby.

More dreams. I am bleeding, not heavily, but not exactly spotting either. I try to call the nurse, to no avail. It is late when I arrive at the hospital. The day is done. She is irritated. "Are you really bleeding or just spotting?" she asks. I feel guilty, embarrassed that I am not sure, that I may be overly worried.

1 marzo

My skin has broken out in a desperate rash. This morning I awaken to a narrow band of pain just below my ribcage. I feel my uterus expanding. I know the baby is larger now. Its presence is irrevocable, and the gravity of this change hits a deeper level. I go back to bed hoping the pain will subside. It does. I awaken to the sound of the boiling kettle. Ella is up.

I think of how my baby will be born in the year of Myrtha's mother's death. I never got to meet her, never got to Puerto Rico as I had promised. Instead, the woman came to me in a dream last night and spoke the name of Refugia. Is this the name of my daughter? But Refugia was a distant bisabuela with hazel eyes and Indian trenzas. I never met her, either, born and buried in the Sonoran century preceding me. Possibly she spoke to me of refugio, that she was seeking some, or that

*I needed to take refuge, find sanctuary some place other than where I
had been looking. Or maybe she wanted me to shelter her youngest
and aging daughter, my Myrtha. And the cycle continues.*

2 marzo

*The results of the CVS test are in. Ella and I are on extension phones
as we hear the genetic specialist tell us the baby is a boy. "That's good
news, isn't it?" she asks. I smile weakly. "Yes, of course. Yes, thank you."
We hang up. Speechless.*

The day before, the specialist left word on the answering machine that the test had shown the baby to be perfectly normal ge-
netically. I didn't realize how worried I had been until I replayed
the recording and burst into tears. I didn't know I had been holding
my breath for those first twelve weeks, fearing to tell anyone I was
pregnant (outside my closest circle of comadres) in the event the
baby would not be healthy. After all, I was forty years old and pregnant for the first time. So the question of the baby's sex came later,
as an afterthought, when one has the luxury to ruminate over such
details.

I confess the news of a baby boy came as a shock to both of us,
probably even more so to Ella who—having grown up the only girl
among four brothers, worked as a firefighter, and raised a gender-
bending male teenager for a time—feels her "male karma" had been
thoroughly fulfilled. (Well, I guess not.) Naive as it may seem, we
believed we were getting a girl, if for no other reason than we had
done the insemination early in my cycle (too early, really) for me to
get pregnant. The reasoning was that I was rushing off for a week
in New York, at the end of which I was to be ovulating. Rather than
waiting another full month, Ella, Pablo, and I decided to get the
"virgin voyage," so to speak, over with. When I learned I was pregnant, I figured all the Y chromosomes had long ago taken their

leave since they are fast swimmers of short duration. I figured wrong. In the end, I realized science had nothing to do with it. This baby was a soul wanting to get here, as a male. Punto final. Later Ella asks, "What will you name him?" "Rafael," I answer, no doubt in my mind. I have always loved the name.

Ella suggests we go to the local bookstore to look up the name to see what message it might bring. In The Book of Saints, *I find Rafael listed among the other Archangels. "The healing power of God," it states. "Patron of musicians and travelers." "Perfect," I say aloud. And I am more reconciled as I see at the bottom of the listing that Rafael Angel's feast day falls on my expected delivery date. September 29. Okay, I say to myself, I get it. Es el destino.*

Upon hearing the news of my baby boy, Myrtha tells me, "He will have a feminine soul."

18 marzo

Ella calls from work and tells me Tede is sick with AIDS. *It is news I have been resisting for three days. A rumor, I told myself. But today it is confirmed, and I think only of the other news, of the boy I am to birth. There is meaning in the fact that my fetus has formed itself into a male, a meaning I must excavate from the most buried places in myself, as well as from this city, this era of dying into which my baby will be born. I understood the female, the daughter. The son holds a message I will learn to decipher with my heart.*

I don't understand dying. I don't understand Tede's dying. My first thought, so selfish—I can't bear to endure another AIDS death. My brief acquaintance with it with Rodrigo** left me mute, horrified. It is

*Tede Matthews was a San Francisco-based Nicaragua solidarity worker, queer poet, and community organizer.
**Chicano joto poet and politico, founder of CURAS, the first AIDS organization in San Francisco specifically for Latino gay men.

not the death that frightens so, it is the slow humiliating dissolution of the body. I fear the face of death. I am ashamed of my fear.

The sun passes through my bedroom window and I find hope in its afternoon warmth. I pray my baby feels it too upon his face and frail chest of pale skin. All day today I have been unable to write. The news of conceiving a son has shaken me profoundly. I toss the coins. The I Ching oracles: "God has manifested himself." The destiny that is joining this boy-child and me and Ella together is out of my hands, and I open my heart to receive him. I name him Rafael Angel...por vida.

19 marzo

Last night, in sweating sleeplessness, I feared my baby was leaving me. I feared the fevers from this flu were burning him out. I feared there was no place for my reckoning with his maleness. I spoke with him all night last night. I spoke to him for understanding amid aching joints and a low-grade fever and a steady dampness between my thighs. I tossed and turned with images of Medea. I still know that this is the play I must write, although I fear it. How is it I can be pregnant and write the story of killing a child? La Llorona. I must believe that my son can forgive his mother's relentless need to describe the source of our female deformation. It is not mere feminist rhetoric that makes a woman stop dumbfounded in the face of a life of raising a son. It is the living woman-wound that we spend our lives trying to heal.

This sickness es una limpieza, I tell myself. These sweats, my own curative waters. "I wanted a female to love," I tell Pablo. He answers, "You've done that your entire life as a lesbian." Yes.

I awaken rested, cooled. It is an overcast morning, and I hear the little neighbor-girl, Morgan, descend the steps from upstairs, chatting endlessly to her mother as she does every morning on her way to school. This morning I hear her voice as a small boy's voice, and it is equally tender.

22 marzo

Last night, a miserable night without sleep, unable to breathe. Spring has arrived, along with my allergies. My body is thick with fatigue. Ella and our neighbor, Ski, dig up the garden, stir up new life after months of rain. I wait for this wave of illness to pass so I can return to work, so I can give my attention to the growing child within me.

At times I fear he has fallen asleep for good. I worry my own fears will turn him bitter against me. I do not feel Rafael Angel as some formless entity that I will shape with my own hands and love. He enters this planet, a soul intact. Who is this being? Some days I imagine him a bitter old man, un juez, severe and authoritative. I imagine him judging my harshness, my moods, my mean ways. At other times, I feel him a young sage-spirit, as delicate as his angelic name.

1 abril

I've returned to New York.

Last time I was here, I was—without knowing—newly pregnant. This morning I am very pregnant...and alone. I put my fingers to a vague and lingering nostalgia for a life ten years ago (my New York days, New York lovers) and remember. But it is no past woman I discover there, more the eruption of who I am today. How do I describe that at the moment of orgasm, I feel the infant inside me curl up into a hard fist, no violence, but a hard ball of intensity swelling in my womb? And I cry for this life, this miracle, this sexuality that is happening to me unlike any I have experienced. The slightest contact evokes a response. Touching myself, remembering touching Ella touching me.

My body is not in this room. It is in a cave somewhere, somewhere dark, somewhere fecund. Soy mujer de barro. Dirt in the creases of my flesh, between my toes, beneath my tongue. The animal kicks inside me, and that's all the sign of life I need. I am female essence relieved of

all burden. There is nothing else required of me but to dwell here,
pregnant. I make love to it, the life.

5 abril

> *"She knew that beauty and bearing witness to the*
> *harsh materials of human struggle need never con-*
> *tradict each other."*
> Adrienne Rich at Audre Lorde's Memorial

I didn't attend Audre's Memorial. I was not among the hundreds that
came from all parts of the country to the Cathedral of St. John the
Divine to give tribute to this woman of genius, heart, and courage.
But I find myself there, there amid that "sacred geometry," months
later on this bitterly cold Saturday afternoon. Sitting in a hard-backed
chair on the stone floor of the largest gothic cathedral in the world, I
pay my own small tribute to Audre Lorde.

In one of the wings of the cathedral, I find an alcove with a small
altar and kneeler dedicated to those who have died of AIDS. Passing
it, I see a dozen or so candles flicker on an otherwise bare prayer
space. I go back to the entrance of the church where I buy a seven-day
votive and return to the alcove. I pray for Tede, maricón, marxista
now sick with SIDA. I pray for my own personal list of HIV-positive
sisters and brothers: Margarita, Imani, Ronnie, José. And I pray for
June and Pat and Merle—and, of course, for Audre—sister-poets gone
and surviving with cancer.

8 abril/Back in San Francisco

I don't know what makes me cry, except the weight of all this change.
I dream that my baby turns out whiter than I expected, but beautiful
still, and talking too soon. I never got to hear his first word. Was it

mami, papi, flor? *Was it* truth? *This baby is already walking and talking full sentences, and I lament that I have missed something in his growing.*

Now I am putting the laundry into sorted piles. I go to the washroom to discover that there is no detergent and Ella is to blame. No one is to blame, but I must blame someone, for some one thing not going as planned. We fight. Ridiculous. She leaves for work and I barely let pass the sound of her tires on the gravel driveway before I am buried, face into the pillow, and weeping. My womb pressed up against the stiff mattress, I feel a slight fluttering and I know the tears are only about this, this overwhelming pending change in our lives. I would never want to go back now, childless. But I wonder about our future. I make room for the baby and am overwhelmed by every box of baby hand-me-downs consuming the space necessary for his arrival. There is no detergent when I need to wash the clothes. I cry.

9 abril

A small cup-sized baby has erupted from my womb in my dream. It has dark hair and what seems like painted black lines for emerging features. The tiny sack of baby hangs by a cord between my legs. I keep trying to push it back inside, knowing it is not yet ready to emerge.

I dream, again. Someone old has passed on. It is not a tragic death because the age is ripe for dying. Upon hearing the news, I receive long green-stemmed flowers of some kind. They will soon blossom yellow and creative. I know it is my baby.

Upon wakening, I go to the bathroom and find myself spotting more heavily than I have since the beginning of my pregnancy. It is a thick earth-brown color. I panic, then try to calm myself. I lie here in bed and ask my baby to give me a sign of life, a fluttering so I know all is well.

10 abril

I am the moon's keeper. Vigilant at 4:00 A.M., the moon rises. I dawn nocturnal. She appears in trinity, each reflection a bit more ephemeral. I rise, search out her light in peopleless bedrooms, through half-open shades. The garden is afternoon-illuminated, and the vegetables, too, grow like babies. In the distance there is the baby-morning cry of a backyard cat, a city rooster's complaint. It is already dawning in San Cristóbal, I think, and remember walking at 5:00 A.M. to its small bus station. I am not now as I once was, that orphaned woman walking the cobblestones in the predawn silence. I am she who rises en busca de la luna, seeking mother/daughter, seeking light.

Moon keeper, I divine.

11 abril

There are days when I am afraid of life hurting us, the homophobia, the racism. When I hear of my brother (today is his birthday) asking my sister, "Was it artificial insemination or did she just get together with some guy?" the harshness in his tone chills me. Is it anger? Fear? What he wants to know is: Who is the father? Where is the man in the picture? The chasm I would have to transverse to have my brother understand who I am in this is too daunting. How can I explain what brought me to the decision to find a man—a decent young man, already a part of my familia—and not ask him to father, but to simply help me get pregnant and be a friend to my child if he could. "I would never speak badly of you to my child," I told Pablo. "What you're giving us is all I want from you. It's enough."*

(Of course, once Rafaelito was born, it was not enough—for any of us. Pablo has always respected the centrality of Ella and me as Rafa's parents, but Pablo's own relationship to Rafael and to "fatherhood" has grown as organically as Rafa himself. Pablo and his family have become family to me and my son. And as family—Ella, Pablo, and I work out our evolving roles and our evolving consciousness in the midst of an evolving child.)

12 abril

I can't get to the heart of my feeling here. I watch my body change daily and know I am not fully residing in it. These miserable allergies are dragging me down into a fog of anxiety, depression. The days are gorgeous, but I cannot fully appreciate them, the winds stirring up the pollen, the seeds of life. Pregnancy happening everywhere and ironically my body is reacting against it. I cling to Ella in a way I never imagined.

13 abril

It is impossible to concentrate on anything but this sudden exposure. I announce my pregnancy to my "Indígena as Scribe" writing class, and immediately I am surrounded by shock and excitement and consejo: "You must get your water filtered." "You have to be smudged in the delivery room. It freaks the hospital staff out cuz the smoke alarms can go off." "Call my mother, la partera, she'll deliver your baby." All good women, concerned women, all thoroughly Indian in their response to me.

I wonder why it is during these times that I am drawn to myth over and over again; possibly it is this research on Heart of the Earth. *In the Indígena class I write, "On the first day of mourning, the men whose hairiness I inherited arrived in canoes with houses built upon them in search of the 'sun's excrement.'" Somehow my giving birth involves me in this trajectory, this continuing history of conquests and culture clashes, of the regeneration of raza and the creation of new razas.*

Nation. Nationality. I am to be the mother of a Mexican baby. I am the worst and best of those macho Chicano nationalists. I picked a man for his brains and dark beauty. And the race continues. But mostly I picked him because I knew he loved me without wanting me. A gay man. A queer contract. And I gotta whitegirl lover with lovely cullud girl curls and a butt to match and Spanish that don't make a fool outta her. This is my home. For now. I don't know what the future will bring. We try to get what we can on paper, to protect ourselves against pain, against loss, but the papers don't protect us. Neither can a nation. Not yet.

17 abril

This is no dream. Bleeding buckets between my legs as I drive to the hospital, my future without this child rushes before me. I try to stop my thoughts: how familiar childlessness is to me; how much simpler it would be; how every corpuscle in my body resists a return to that state.

When I get to the Kaiser clinic, I go straight into the staff area, looking for Nurse Eileen. "She's gone for the day," they say. "But I'm bleeding," I respond. And then I hear her voice. "Cherríe, is that you?" She enters the room, her round freckled face wrinkling into a frown. When I see her, I am no woman, no future, no thought. I am all-present, all girl-child with baby, and I cry to her, "I'm bleeding." She rushes me into an examination room and feels for the baby with groping hands. At that point of contact, I feel my baby move up to meet her open palms. I know my baby is whole and complete inside. No miscarriage, the heavy bleeding due to polyps sloughing off from the cervix.

Since the bleeding—how to describe it? I am homebound and, ironically, read daily of Maya ritual bloodletting, of shamans and diviners. I remain ever awed by the fragility of the life inside me, or maybe it is only I who am fragile. At each threat to my pregnancy, the baby remains sólido, intacto. His heartbeat growing in resonance, conviction, full human-beingness. What relief to hear it beating without disturbance next to my frantically beating heart as Nurse Eileen put the heart monitor to my womb.

I have no control over this vulnerability. I tell Myrtha it is so hard to want something so bad and to feel that this destiny of mother and child is truly out of my hands, truly a gift from the cosmos. I am here to receive it, but I cannot cling to it any more than I can predict the nature of the son I will have. I keep thinking he is his own soul, so much so that at times I forget my own role in shaping him. My friends remind me. "You will make a wonderful mother," they say. Even some have said how lucky Rafael Angel will be to have me as his mother. And this shocks me each time in the hearing. He is all gift to me. But they tell me I also am a gift to my son. All my relations.

25 abril

I return from the "Ceremony"* at Bear Camp. I look for an opening of understanding about my experience there: thirty hours without sleep; the preference given to males throughout la ceremonia—they, the firekeepers, the pipecarriers, the jefes. Lying on my bed, the afternoon sun spills over the bedspread and I sleep heavily. When I awaken, I am convinced that there is some ritual of closing I still need to perform. I rise, wash all my clothes, clean my car of the earth and mud, my hair and body of smoke, fire, and fatigue.

This writing is part of that closing, that opening, that continuance of what touched me somehow, unwittingly, in these last days of pure offering. Not that my spirit was pure, only there was no other way to

---

*A Native American sacred ritual that may involve a number of days of fasting, sweats, prayer, and "medicine." In recent years, many Chicana/os have begun to regularly attend Ceremony as part of their own religious observance.

understand the weekend, except to see it as an offering. All was discomfort, working when what I was needing was rest, waiting on men (which I found distasteful), the intensity of the heat from the sweat lodge (this I wanted), the endless hours of sitting in ceremony, unable to stretch my cramped legs and spasming back, fighting back a constant call to sleep.

But there were revelations minute by minute. During la ceremonia, as others suffered separation around me, I did not feel alone. Holding my womb, I rocked and rocked, and my son and I spoke secrets to each other in the circle of the fire. (I may never feel this "unalone" again, I thought.) I prayed and dozed off into mundane dreams of steak dinners and other small cravings, then would awaken to pray some more. I prayed that I would learn how to raise a male child well, that the wounds men have inflicted on me, even in their absence, will not poison me against my son.

I did not have the histories so many of the folks present at the ceremony claimed: drug abuse, poverty, violent relationships, "skid row." My battles, challenges, have always been more invisible. But it is with that history and this baby inside that I proceed. I ask for light. I thank the spirit for what has already been freely given.

Son to his mother at the Ceremony: "You can lead a horse to water. You have led me to the river, it's up to me if I'm gonna drink."

There is no closure, only this beginning, my return to Heart of the Earth with new eyes, my return to Ella with renewed love, understanding. I have this life inside me to thank for the generosity his presence has brought to our relationship. Seeing Ella's goodness to me in my pregnancy has opened my heart to her in a way I know cannot be reversed. She has allowed me to depend on her. And, for the first time in my life, I do.

27 abril

Last week, one of my leaders died, Cesar Chavez. I cut the grainy newsprint photo from the already-yellowing daily paper. The caption reads: "He grew up in tar-paper shacks." It is a sad picture: Cesar's forced half-smile, eyes looking off to the side hooded by aging indio eyelids, a full head of near-white hair. He is not wholly present in the photo, his heart somewhere else. It shows. I scotchtape the image onto the white wooden wall behind my altar and notice Audre's photo beneath it: her arms outstretched in a communal embrace, her full body draped in an African robe. She has a radiant smile.

I don't know if Audre and Cesar ever met each other, but between them the story of my own political history as a Chicana and a lesbian is told. A decade ago Audre and I left New York and drifted apart. I had returned to my homeland in California, the land of Cesar's movement, and Audre had returned to her island in the Caribbean.

Since Audre's passing, I've begun to try and speak to her again. It is easier now, the geographical distance no longer of consequence. It is also easier, I think, because the living always presume the wisdom of those who have passed on, their infinite capacity for understanding, their generosity of spirit. Audre: the first ancestor of my own colored lesbian tradition.

Tell me about freedom now, sister-poet. Teach me.

In Audre and Cesar's passing, the proximity of their deaths to each other, I wonder about leadership. Who is there to replace them?

Cesar died in his sleep, a tired man. In conversation with a friend, she tells me she fears he died of a broken heart. We'll never know. He died suddenly...after thirty years of lucha and no re-emerging movimiento on the horizon. I remember reading, years ago, about Emma Goldman's death in the 1930s, how after a lifetime of devoted anarchism, the woman died watching fascism take root in Europe. She, too, may have died of a broken heart.

But not Audre.

28 mayo

A full month since I've last written. I dream that Ella and I are at a botánica. The walls are lined with jars of herbs and medicines from floorboard to ceiling. I don't know what our illness is, or the remedy. I do not feel ill. A beautiful boy of about nine approaches. He is the son of Ella's friend. We say her name in greeting him. He is the essence of life itself, a beautiful brown face, huge eyes, thick dark hair. He exudes a genuine kindness. I wonder, upon waking, is he my son?

30 mayo

I can't write sitting up in bed anymore. My belly's too big. The baby moves around constantly now, especially when I am resting or sitting still. He is a fish inside me, flapping his tail, gulping down the waters of my womb. He is pure animal, nothing human about these sensations. They are the animal I am when I make love, am hungry, move my bowels, fall into a deep unconscious sleep.

Hours ago, Dorothy was here with her nine-month-old baby and her lover. We ate well, conversed lightly, the baby drawing most of our attention. Dorothy spoke briefly of her new novel. Mostly we spoke of the business of writing—the success of Bastard *after so many years of hand-to-mouth subsistence, eking out the time and means to write.* As we spoke, the idea of writing a novel came back to me. Suddenly this baby due, and I realize the vulnerability I feel with my writing career as a playwright and poet. How little money it earns, how hard it is to promote the work. But beyond the financial concerns, I long for that kind of extended involvement in a work. I think, what pleasure to immerse oneself in a single story for a long, long time. I always have the sense that my writing is incomplete somehow—the poems, the plays, the essays—striving at something not wholly realized. Maybe the novel*

*Dorothy Allison's *Bastard Out of Carolina.*

*would allow me that space to explore the deepest concerns. Thoroughly.
I don't know. I write theoretically here when the urge is simply to
create. My body now taking on the full shape of creation does not
lessen my need for art.*

11 junio/New York City

Here again, to work on yet another draft of Heart of the Earth. *I can't
write now because I need to keep my feet up. They have swollen into
Flintstone feet in this New York heat, and my hands grow quickly
numb holding up this book and pen in the air over my belly. All I am
waiting for is to escape this heat, to be rejoined with Ella at her mother's
house on the Cape, to rest.*

18 junio/Cape Cod

*I awaken this morning as an expectant mother, worrying. I don't
know if it is the pregnancy or allergies again that cause me to want so
much sleep. I take two-hour naps, stay up till midnight, sleep again
till 10:00 A.M.*

*The baby greets me with bolder movement each day. I feel him now
just to the right of my navel. I dream his future face nightly. I feel a
slight muscle spasm in the left side of my neck and imagine my baby
has traveled up there, stirring everywhere throughout my body.*

*Hormones. I cry freely and without will or censor. Last night I go to
bed, weepy-eyed when Ella comes in. We have just seen a show about
transgenders. Since the featured male-to-female started out heterosexual, I suggest that her sexuality (attraction to women) will remain
the same after her operation and she will become a lesbian. Ella's
mother is mind-boggled. "But they made her a vagina with feeling.
After all that, how could she still want to be with a woman?" I respond,*

"I have a vagina with feeling and I want to be with a woman." She goes silent. Later when Ella comes back into the room, we argue about numbers: what percentage of transgenders becomes straight, what relationship sexuality has to transgenderism. The "debate" is not the point. I am hurt by her mother's response. She is not being mean—my mother would unwittingly have said (or at least thought) the same. But I wonder how it is that although Ella and I are present as partners every day in front of her mother, and at night Ella and I make a purposeful and impassioned love, still, in her mom's mind, sex has to be with a penis. Ella misunderstands my sadness, my hormone-induced tears. She complains of my man-hating, my dick-centered resentment (envy). I go to sleep wallowing in my queer sense of isolation/alienation even from my lesbian lover. She's a femme, I think. She doesn't really understand.

19 junio

Ella tells me daily how much more feminine I look. I see it, too—my hair longer than it's been in fifteen years, my hips and thighs and breasts rounding from this pregnancy, the softening taking place throughout my body, the tears. I like it and yet in bed feel a strong urge to reassert my butchness, my self as a love-maker.

As I feel myself enlarging in open-heartedness, in body, I feel closer to Ella than ever. "The stakes are higher now," I tell her, "the sex has got to meet that heart place." I tell her how frightening that can be for me, that nakedness. "We are so different," she responds. It is a statement of faithfulness, I know, when it is that face-to-face nakedness she craves. And I have faith too, although I cry. I cry because I know this is another step into a deepening between us, the terrain of which is as unfamiliar as this baby. After four years, how does one continue loving? What does it look like?

21 junio

Summer solstice finds the Cape—a heavy, hot, grey cloud pressing down upon its grey citizens. But there is an unparalleled beauty here. It lies in the waveless sea.

Yesterday. Ella and I go to the beach. We stop first at the bathroom. She is in the stall next to me. I very methodically cut strips of toilet paper to line the toilet seat before I sit (the way my mother taught me as a child). Just as I start to sit down, I look up and see Ella has been watching me, her head peeking over the stall wall. In jest, she has put on a monster's face, sticking out her tongue, twisting her mouth, and rolling her eyes up into her head. I am so startled that, even as she laughs, I break out into deep sobs. Where the fear comes from I don't know. I am amazed and relieved by the tears, how completely I experience everything these days. Later, when Ella inadvertently bumps a tree in the parking lot as she backs the car out, I scream at her. I am primordial protection. I am afraid that my baby has been jolted, afraid of what could have happened with a harder knock, a crash. I cry.

I have a vague sense that I dreamed last night I had given birth prematurely. Again. He is only in his sixth month, and I worry that his lungs are not yet fully developed enough to survive on his own.

22 junio

> *"But after you hear the story, you and the others prepare by the new moon to rise up against the slave masters."*
> Leslie Marmon Silko, Almanac of the Dead

I lose the thread, the purpose of the writing, until I am reminded by Leslie Marmon Silko's words that a story can cause revolt. That is my sole purpose, arrogant as it may seem, to write those kinds of stories,

stories to agitate, stories to remind us what has been forgotten. These days I doubt my capacity to do that. I wonder if that feeling ever goes away in the life of the writer. There in the realm of my doubt, the world becomes unbearably small, as small as my pitiful ego. But when I imagine I can speak with the voice of others—that others can speak through me—how wide and hopeful the project of writing becomes again.

A boy of about nine walks by this Cape Cod window. He carries a violin case. He must have an 8:00 A.M. Friday appointment down the dead-end street. He looks neither eager nor sullen about going, only obligatory. Minutes later, the little boy returns by the same path, passes by the window again. He looks fatter upon his return, thoroughly irritated. He swings his free arm heavy with a child's unempowered resentment. Wrong day? Wrong time? Nobody home?

These journal entries are my meager attempts to keep the pen flowing, to discover the next step en la jornada. My road is now open, with Heart of the Earth *on tour in upstate New York, and the play collection off to its publisher.* I feel empty of stories, empty of ideas, words, images, impulses. The creative juices used to fuel this baby's development make my hunger for writing stronger. I shape these letters onto the page as tiny steps in a dance circling circling circling until I arrive at the heartbeat, a pulse, a place from which the writing stirs new life.*

30 junio/Kaiser Hospital, Hollywood

I watch the heart monitor obsessively. It is everything to me. Like religion. All that matters is the stress-free beating of my baby's heart, his kicking signs of life, the steady unwavering pattern of the monitor printout indicating no contractions. But I am awakened at 2:00 A.M.,

---

**Heroes and Saints & Other Plays* (Albuquerque, NM: West End Press, 1994) *a routine check, and am told contractions are seven to eight minutes apart. My world shrinks to the parameter of my thirsty womb as I beg my baby to stay put there, hold on, cling to me incubating as long as possible.*

Twenty-seven weeks is so damn young.

My water broke the day before I was due to return to San Francisco. The date was June 27.

Following my stay in Cape Cod, I had flown to Los Angeles for a brief visit with my family, knowing I probably wouldn't see them again until after the baby's birth in late September. I had gone with my sister's family to Huntington Beach the night before for an evening bonfire, but my brother-in-law had other plans. He wanted to talk, he told me. He actually said he wanted to "find closure," a therapeutic term he had acquired during the three brief visits of couples' counseling he had done with my sister. He had to discuss their impending divorce, bare his soul, and so off we walked down the beach for what seemed like miles. As my brother-in-law talked and talked and talked, I knew this one-way conversation had nothing to do with me and everything to do with him and the image he was working on creating of himself as a responsible, sensitive kind of guy: father, husband, ex-husband, ex-brother-in-law.

The day before that, my sister had pressed on—"Let's go to another mall"—in earnest search of baby paraphernalia. I knew I was slowly beginning to lose it—physically, emotionally. Wait until I get home, I thought. This is the least I can do for people who need me.

But the baby wouldn't wait. The next morning at my parents' house in San Gabriel, suddenly feeling overwhelmingly tired, I excuse myself from the breakfast table. My parents both turn their faces up to me and away from their morning eggs. I had to go back to bed, I told them, just for an hour or so. And they agree rest is what I need. The exhaustion is so sudden, so bottomless as I drag myself off to the closet-sized room that was once my brother's bedroom. The phone rings, just as I feel the rush of warm water bathe

48

my thighs. I know it is Ella. I reach over to the phone, lift up the receiver. "My water just broke," I cry. I am not seven months pregnant. She catches the first flight out of Boston.

After a series of phone calls—between my mom and Ella, Ella and Kaiser, between L.A. and San Francisco and Cape Cod, Ella frantically trying to get the best medical advice for me from three thousand miles away—my parents manage to get me an appointment with a private obstetrician. They lay me carefully onto the back seat of the family car, and when we arrive at the clinic, my father finds a wheelchair to get me up to the third floor. In retrospect, I see now I should have gone directly to emergency, and that's what the doctor says minutes after the sonogram showed my womb virtually empty of amniotic fluid. Merely a small dark pool of liquid remained, not nearly enough to keep a baby afloat. I am horrified as I study the sonogram monitor. My mother stands next to me. "The baby's fine," she says, not fully understanding the signs. I tell her, "It's not good, Mamá. He's too little to be born now."

The ambulance drive from the clinic in Pasadena to Hollywood Kaiser is interminable. I try to "read" the route from the shape of streetlights overhead, the curve of freeway interchanges, the tops of palm and sycamore trees lining the backstreets we travel. My mother is in the front seat with the driver. My father will meet us there in his own car. I make idle chit-chat with the salvadoreño paramedic, but my mouth has dropped somewhere into my womb and I sing only one real song: *Hang on, mijito. Stay inside me, please stay inside me.*

I am flat on my back as I am rolled on a gurney into the labor room. If the baby doesn't come in twenty-four hours, the doctors tell me, he can stay in my womb for weeks, maybe months, even without the fluid. The objective is to keep the baby inside me for as long as possible. I am to remain flat on my back and in the hospital until this baby is born. The next day, Ella arrives. I hadn't realized how much I was needing her until our eyes meet. Her face is the mirror of tenderness, recognition I have been waiting for. She rushes

49

to me. My parents graciously leave us alone, and I cry my child's heart out.

After the initial crisis, it appears that Rafael has decided to hold on for a while. I have had no contractions for twenty-four hours, so I am moved into the maternity ward to homestead. At twenty-seven weeks gestation, they tell us that the baby's lungs are not strong enough to breathe on their own. Ella has already found two books on premature births. She studies them. She explains the risks to me, editing out the worse potential parts of the scenario. Thirty-two weeks is our goal. At thirty-two weeks gestation, the baby can breathe well on his own, the heart duct which is connected to the lungs has closed, and the baby will be small but quite whole and out of danger.

Thirty-two weeks never come, nor does a full twenty-eight. For the next six days the baby remains inside me. My family visits me with vigilance, Ella ever-faithful at my bedside. With every change in my body temperature, every increase or decrease in contractions, I am taken from the maternity ward to delivery and back again. I am visited by a revolving door of neo-natalists, residents, interns, nurses, and nurses aides; but no one seems to be able to clearly answer my questions: How did this happen? I had no infection, no trauma to my womb. What are my baby's chances for survival and a healthy life? One incident I remember vividly is being told off-handedly by a resident (at least fifteen years younger than I), as she did a routine check, that if my baby were to be born right then, it would have a 25 percent chance for survival. Not true, I learn later, but in seconds my temperature shoots up and I am put back on a heart monitor.

3 julio

Rafael Angel is born 3:05 P.M. Full moon.

I am speechless, my child somehow exactly as I had imagined him.

This gift, this messenger, this child who could not wait to enter me, to enter this world. I sleep now to dream of him, dreaming down the hall, a two-pound-six-ounce milagrito, mi bebé.

The intensive part of the labor was short: four hours. I have the nurses call Ella that morning of July third, somehow knowing today would be the day. The doctors still have given me no clear sense of what a twenty-eight-week birth means for my baby's health. I try to push that worry out of my mind; I think only of a safe delivery.

The night before, Ella had stayed with me in the labor room until the early hours of the morning. The contractions were strong enough to feel, but not so strong that I couldn't fall asleep. I finally send her home (my parents' home) for some rest. At 7:00 A.M. I am awake. The contractions are stronger now, still not severe enough to be concerned, I think. I have the nurses call Ella. "Ask her to be here by eleven," I say. Somehow the message gets confused. My mother receives the call, doesn't want to disturb Ella sleeping, but can't figure out if there is a reason to worry. She calls my sister. At eleven, Ella and Jo Ann both magically arrive, independent of one another. That's all I need. Once my sister and lover are here, I know I'm in good hands.

Needless to say, Ella and I never took the natural childbirth classes. Those were to be reserved for those lazy August months when I'd have nothing better to do. My sister, however, was a virtual pro at Lamaze, having given birth to four healthy babies with that method. So, minutes after Jo Ann arrives, she is grilling me with questions about my symptoms. "Where do you feel the pain? How far apart are the contractions?" And Ella is flipping frantically through childbirth books, trying to read about what's going to happen minutes before it's happening. But they make a marvelous delivery team. As the pains increase in intensity, Ella (per Jo Ann's instructions) pushes on my lower back to relieve some of the pain. I have never appreciated Ella's physical strength as I did that day.

No lightweight lover for me, the girl is pure power.

A few hours later, my parents arrive with my Auntie Eva. They are all dressed up y perfumados, coming for a casual hospital visit. Try as I might, I cannot keep face. I am in the throes of labor, and my sister gracefully tells them this is not such a good time for the visit. She'll call when we know anything more. They leave the hospital, a bit disoriented, none of us knowing I would deliver in the next hour.

How could we know? This is my first baby, and during a full week of being taken in and out of the labor room, I had heard my neighbor-laborers screaming at the top of their lungs. "Ay, Mamacita!" "Give me some damn drugs!" "No! No! No!" So I figure that whatever pain I got going (which was the most fierce physical pain I had ever experienced), it has to get worse and I am trying to conserve what energy I have for the long haul. My sister keeps assuring me that a big mouth doesn't necessarily mean bigger pain. Still, I hang on, politely breathing as Jo Ann instructs me, pushing out air in long drags, then short rhythmic puffs. All the while, Ella keeps pressing on my back for a moment of blessed relief, then rushes back to her birthing books. In the meantime, Jo Ann jots down in a little note pad how close the contractions are coming. Now the contractions are one on top of the other and virtually unbearable. My sister suggests I get up on all fours to relieve the pressure on my lower back where the pain is the most severe. The moment I do, I feel a revolution occur in my womb, the pain taking a full somersault inside of me, dropping down into what feels like my bowels. (Thinking about it, I realize that that one move may have saved me hours of labor.) I fall back onto my back, feel the urge to defecate, tell them so. Jo Ann says, "That's the baby." Ella rushes out to get a doctor. The staff has virtually ignored us for the last three hours since every time they checked, the monitor wasn't reading the contractions as intensely as I was experiencing them.

The doctor wastes no time in coming. Since the time my water broke, seven days earlier, I had not been examined vaginally, for fear of infection. No one, therefore, had checked the dilation of my cervix throughout the labor. As the young Asian-American resident is opening my legs, I glance at the clock above her head. Three o'clock. Her hand moves up inside me. "I can feel the head," she says. "Get her into the delivery room."

Now I know what that statement means for a premature baby. Within five minutes, the on-call staff at the Intensive Care Nursery—the neo-natalist, the respiratory therapist, the ICN nurse—will meet us in delivery. Ella and Jo Ann have disappeared. Next time I see them, they are standing on each side of me, wearing pale pink surgical gowns and masks. The doctor tells me to push. And I do. Grabbing my sister's hand on my left side, my lover's on the right, I push with everything I've got. I hear them prompting me on, everybody approving. *Good, good, good.* I push. *That's it, he's coming. Go on.* I push. *There he is, one more.* Ella tells me she can see him. Then the doctor's voice is urgent. *Stop. Don't push. Hold back.* I don't know why. My vagina is pure fire, a horrible burning. When everything in me wants to push him all the way out, they tell me to stop. But it is the cord, the cord is wrapped around his neck. The doctor remains very calm, cuts the baby free. Then I let go and let him spill out of me.

Relief, my body is engulfed in a pleasure—an animal pleasure, a pulsing, an aliveness like nothing I've known. I am a girl and a woman and an animal, and estoy temblando like the best of sex, the best of being thoroughly entered and spent. They don't bring the baby to my belly as they do in the movies. I see out of the corner of my eye a circle of masked strangers around him. They, too, are dressed in pink. I am afraid to look, afraid to know how my baby looks. Is he well? Is he breathing? A final push and the afterbirth spills out of me. I want to keep the cord, bury it somewhere, somewhere far away from this hospital. *How is my baby?*

Then Ella ventures over to him, breaking that tight circle of urgent latexed hands and plastic tubes and blinking monitors. I hear her from the distance, a mere distance of five feet or so, that seems so far away from me. She says, "He has an indio nose." And I cry from relief now. I cry and laugh and tremble with the joy of his birthing. It was the best thing to say. I know he is okay or else she would have said something else. He is okay, alive, whole, born. They rush him out of the delivery room into Intensive Care. I still haven't seen his face.

After a few hours of recovery, Ella and my sister take me over to the ICN. I must admit, I am afraid to go, afraid to see this being whose face my lover has seen but not I, not yet. But when I do see him, he is a miniature of all I understand of beauty. He is the tiniest creature I have ever seen. His skin hangs off of him como un viejito, and there is a thin veil of dark hair coating his body. He is the most beautiful little monkey in the world. I am not shocked to see him. He looks just as I have imagined him, but his fragility is almost unfathomable. How do I protect him from so far away?

That night, after Ella leaves, I consider what has brought me—now us—to this place in time. In a way, the most natural thing in the world was to give birth here in Los Angeles, among my blood familia. I knew as I held my lover's and my sister's hands in the grip of labor that this was what I understood as hogar, sustenance; that this is how a woman should always give birth, surrounded by women. And how lucky I was to be a lesbian, to have it all—mother, sister, lover—that family of women to see me into motherhood. I couldn't help but think I had willed it in some way, to give birth to Rafael Angel in the City of the Angels.

II
Waiting in the Wings

I've never before experienced the feeling
of having to physically keep Death away,
as if he would actually come in the door
if I let down my guard for an instant.

Paul Monette, *Borrowed Time*

Nothing will ever be the same.

I knew our lives would be changed by the arrival of this baby, but the manner of his arrival is as nothing I have known in my life, feeling so awestruck by every moment—Rafaelito's push toward life.

I am afraid to write of these times, afraid somehow language will lessen what I know.

7 julio/San Gabriel

Today as I fight off the traces of a cold, I focus on nothing else but purifying myself, so that when Rafaelito begins to draw from my milk tomorrow, it will fortify him, sustain him as his life-struggle sustains me. This child is no stranger to me—possibly because he looks now as he will look eighty years from now, an old man, I already gone. I see in him my mother's aging forehead, my own collapsing chin (once perfectly delineated), the blurring ancient eyes of my grandmother in the years just before her death at ninety-six. But my son's life lies before him, and each day the ancientness will obscure itself in ounces of baby fat. He will carry this knowledge of this closeness to death, the other side of life, as a great secret inside of him.

Today I do not visit him. I take the day to recuperate, but every time I close my eyes he is visible right behind my eyelids, an image pressed upon my memory, my sleeping and waking life. My mind does not always serve as my friend. My heart, yes. In that place resides a seamless connection between my baby's essence beating inside those incubator walls and my milk-hard-breasted body. I struggle to overcome this constant fear and anxiety in the effort to discover a deep and unwavering faith in his survival, his fruitfulness, his life.

8 julio

My faith has been challenged. Faith in what? The benevolence of the universe? To whom do I pray? To the dispassionate face of the Indian Virgen who must know something of what I suffer—she who bore a son, who lost a son? To the broken body of an Aztec lunar goddess that I witnessed whole and womanly two Mexican summers past? Is it her strength—the power of Coyolxauhqui—I draw from, a female power potent enough to eclipse the sun? Or is it the Califas ocean, swelling into a rage yet tender enough to sustain a child's blue balloon afloat for hours? I follow the balloon with my eyes as it dances at the precipice of the breaking waves. These are the ruminations of a fully grown, fully unfearful woman. That is not me.

At forty, I feel myself respond to the crisis of Rafaelito's sudden entrance into this world as I did as a child of eight fearing my mother's death. At eight, I prayed endlessly all night long as my mother lay in a hospital bed some fifteen miles away. I dug a crater into the inside of my elbow with nervous nails, scratching scratching scratching. I worried. I worried for her life. I grew superstitious, feared the wrong set of prayers, a forgotten passage, a misdirected look at a plaster saint could mean her death. I prayed and feared always God's punishment, God's closed ears and heart. I kept my sister up at night. I cried. Today my mother said to me, "Remember, hija, it was your prayers that got me out of the hospital." She, too, thought of the child I was thirty-two years ago.

Now, I see faith is not so easy to secure. I am still superstitious as I pour my breast milk, as offering, into the garden earth. I fear the wrong gesture, the wrong words might offend those ever-heartless gods. I take the chance anyway, watering the garden with my body's milk. I pray as I pour—for life, for my son's life.

As I see Rafaelito grow stronger and healthier each day, I can't make sense of my blessing in the face of the ailing babies next to him, barely clinging to life, hooked up to respirators and IVs. When my mother and I go to Sears to buy nursing bras and newborn infant wear (clothes Rafaelito cannot possibly fit into for months), she tells the young Chicana cashier about my preemie baby boy. The cashier tells us of her brother, also born premature, now thirteen with a cleft palate and seizures. "He's only grown up to here." She measures the air, stopping at her elbow. I fear hearing her speak of it, fear bad omens lying dormant in strangers' anecdotes. My mother confesses the same fear to me. Coming out of the store into the low-hanging L.A. smog, she says, "When I was pregnant, I thought it wasn't good to even look at a deformed child."

My faith has been challenged. I have never been so close to and so afraid of death as I have been with the emergence of my son into the world. How does one have faith when one is consumed by fear? I have felt this way since the moment my water broke without warning ten days ago. But as I held him for the first time today, my hand wrapping fully around the small birdweight of his head, all was life. He is thoroughly present, his blue-black eyes taking me in. "Sí, soy tu madre," I say. He is as near to me as when he kicked inside me, and I am filled with hope and promise for our lives together. Maybe Rafaelito will bring to me a more profound way of believing. Rafael: "the healing power of God," I remember. Maybe he is my teacher.

9 julio

I dream that my son has been born but is not fully human in form yet. He is a kind of guzanito in the early stages of development. How gratified I was to awaken to the memory of his perfectly human face staring back at me from my arms.

In another dream, I am to attend some kind of gathering of women, a kind of retreat. When I arrive, I am shocked to see mostly white women dressed in ethnic fabrics. I can't keep face. I don't want to be here. I want to find my sister. I cry and cry and want to return only to my baby's side. I can think of nothing else. Later in the same dream I am on the phone debating with a man, then a woman, over their rights to a piece of my writing. "I don't give a damn," I tell them. "I'll return the payment to you. Don't use my work." I cry to my mother, "I care about nothing but this baby." She understands.

About five days after Rafa's birth, Ella goes home to San Francisco to "get things in order." The plan is that she will return in a week, and that we will spend the summer here in Los Angeles until the baby is well and grown enough to return with us to San Francisco. We will sublet an apartment and move our work south for the time being (at least two to three months, they tell us). Rafael Angel's condition has been stable so far, his breathing normal, with the occasional bradycardias* when he "forgets" to breathe. The nurses tell us it is normal, his premature system not yet in full operation. I am awed that even the instinct to breathe is not a given. Rafaelito is also too young to suck. For at least the next five weeks he will be fed my breast milk through a tube down his throat. So I pump and label and store my milk in the hospital freezer and in my parents' freezer, transporting it in small ice chests each day to the ICN. As I watch the soft white liquid descend through the tube into his pursed mouth, I tell him, "One day, hijo, te daré el pecho. Ten paciencia." More for myself than him.

14 julio

Rafael is transported by air ambulance to San Francisco Kaiser. We are not home yet.

I arrive one morning at the ICN to be told, without warning, that Rafaelito is stable enough to be transferred to San Francisco

---

*Excessively slow heartbeat rate.

Kaiser. "Is it safe?" I ask. Yes, they tell me, explaining that a nurse, a doctor, and a respiratory therapist will fly down from San Francisco to travel with him. I call Ella right away, tell her, "Don't bother coming down. We're coming home."

The hospital plane is waiting as we pull up in the ambulance. Rafaelito is rolled aboard in a compact incubator with all the necessary accouterments: heart monitor, oxygen saturation monitor, IV in place, respirator ready to go just in case. Nurse Bobbie from San Francisco Kaiser is a mixed blessing, cracking jokes the entire way about *Ra-fee-el* already being a jet-setter, playing stewardess as she passes out plastic-wrapped sandwiches and beverages. She relieves me of some of my anxiety, but is a bit more blonde cheerleader than my mood. Still, when she asks if Ella will be there to meet me, referring to her by name, my heart opens to her. She's read the report, I think. She knows we are dykes, and I am relieved that we will have at least one emissary at this new hospital. One less thing to explain. The doctor, a thin, bearded Jewish neo-natalist, has little to say to me throughout the trip. As I gaze out the porthole window, the view moving from farmland to forest, I hear him making copious notes next to me, his pen scratching against the clipboard. I glance over to the report on his lap, spot the words *artificial insemination*. Everybody knows my business, I think, and I remember how un-"artificial" that moment felt to me. Then I ask him, "So, what do you think, Doctor? How's the baby gonna do?" He answers, almost disappointed, "Oh, this baby's not even a challenge." I think that is supposed to encourage me, but weeks later, when Rafael is being taken into surgery barely clinging to life, I want to ask him, "Challenge enough for you now, Doc?"

19 julio

> *"This time is a subtle study in non-action as a way of attaining real meaning in your life."*
> I Ching

No truer words. I am in the hospital cafeteria again. These days are the hard days. Rafaelito back on a ventilator, blood transfusion yesterday, twenty-four hours nonstop bradycardias. Today he is stable but exhausted. I am exhausted, too, have never lived like this before. It takes great effort to move this pen across the page in an attempt to document some thread of what I am/we are experiencing. To document my son's survival. "Guerrero," I call him. Warrior boy.

Tede died yesterday. Without his knowing, he has been an intimate part of Rafaelito's life. Tede writing me of angels, never knowing I held one with folded wings inside of me. My choosing Angel for Rafaelito's second name. Hearing that Tede had AIDS so close to the news of Rafael's boyhood/maleness. Is there a kind of queer balance to this birthing and dying...lesbians giving life to sons, our brothers passing? He is the child of queers, our queer and blessed family, laughing with Pablo and Ella after the insemination, sitting on the bed next to me. We just laughed and laughed.

Rafaelito came to me effortlessly, our first try at conception. He was, literally, waiting in the wings...angel wings, waiting for me to finally decide to call him to this earth. But now I see Rafaelito is not so easily won. He enters this life with a delicate deep strength, as living reminder of the precariousness of our lives. I breathe through the isolette, call to him, to me, to us, to life. "Rafaelito, Rafaelito, quédate aquí, hijo, con nosotros. Tu familia te espera." I call him over to this side.

It is hard to write, harder yet to pray.

I am now in the Intensive Care Nursery. Rafaelito se ve tan pálido. They tell me not to touch him today, to let him rest, but I want him to know I am here. I do not touch. I watch. I watch his small ribcage rise and fall, sometimes with such great effort. Then when his chest is still, I search the monitors frantically, always in momentary panic that mi hijo may have forgotten again to breathe. At this hour of the late afternoon, his chest appears almost transparent. Ella arrives.

20 julio

Ella called the hospital this morning to inquire about the baby, having to put up with the usual deterrents: "Who are you?" The receptionist hears no male voice on the line, but a woman, my lover, seeking to know about our son. "Read the damn chart," Ella snaps back. "I'm the co-mother." Co-mother—*a concept about which even San Francisco hospitals haven't a clue. I cannot comfort Ella much when she is bruised by the hospital's ignorance. I hear only her telling me Rafaelito has had more "bradys." "How many?" I want to know and do not want to know and suffer that I am not there with him at this moment and suffer that I also can hardly bear to see him struggle so to breathe. And still we don't know what's wrong with him.*

Ella and I will split shift tomorrow—me, in the day, she, in the evening—so he won't be left alone without us. We draw comfort seeing him together, but it seems there is little room for comfort these days.

I learn the lessons of motherhood daily. There are no guarantees, only faith. But what is there to believe in other than simply Rafaelito was destined to come into this life and share it for a time with us? How I want that time to be full and long and rich. How desperately I want his survival as I have wanted nothing before in my life. I pray for this as minute by minute Rafaelito struggles simply to remember to breathe.

21 julio

"Something's not right with this kid, Doc." It is Nurse Rose who insists and persists. It is Ella who stands sentinel next to her. She, too, insists on answers. Now. What is happening to our child? I sit by Rafaelito's isolette, motionless. I am riveted to the chair. I have no voice, only that same silent mantra inside my heart. Quédate aquí, hijo. Quédate. *The monitors indicating bradycardias are going off dozens of times a minute now. And with each alarm, I feel my heart jolt. With each jolt, Ella and I lock eyes. Are we losing our son?*

The doctor-on-call is not responding: that same nonchalant neo-natalist I met on that hospital plane one week ago. "Something is not right with this kid, Doc," Rose insists. Again. At first they think it is pneumonia. They take a chest X-ray. Nada. An inaccurate image. They take another and, by chance, a partial picture of the intestines can be seen. There is a small dark spot.

24 julio

I didn't write when the days were the worst, when they rolled his tiny isolette down the corridor into surgery and Rafaelito followed our sad gaze (a calm recognition in his eyes) until he was out of sight. I didn't write when they told us the hardest words to hear, "If it is too late, we'll just close him up again." Our baby had contracted NEC, the thing we most feared, an infection that literally eats up the intestine, deadly among many preemies.

In the waiting room one floor below surgery, we wait for some word. Pablo has just left, or rather we sent him away, somehow knowing Ella and I needed to be alone in this, needed to find a private way to stave off this baby's passing. I have brought a rosary, the wooden one given to me by my mother. Ella and I wrap ourselves up together in the deep vinyl lounge chair, we hold each other and pray. "Dios te salve, María..."

You were there, weren't you, Tede? Irish and ancestor. Our queer recently born ancestor with all the dead Mexican relatives we remembered and invoked. Abuelita, who always asked me, "¿Cuando te vas a casar, hija? Necesitas familia." While my family held me in her lion arms and my son had his guts cut open on the floor just above our heads.

In the midst of our prayer, I realize suddenly—so profoundly—

that my tightest hold against death cannot keep Rafaelito here. The holding itself is what Rafaelito does not need. He needs to be free to decide: to stay or to leave. Oh, how I hoped he would stay, but I couldn't make it happen. I only knew my clinging so tightly to my son's waning life could surely crush him and all the heart I had; and there would be no heart left to either mourn or raise a son. I can't explain the feeling, that moment of saying to Ella, against every instinct in me, "We gotta let go." Wasn't it our vigilance that was keeping him here? In the letting go might he not slip from us completely? That was the risk, for what did we two know of death in this most intimate way?

"Si es tu voluntad." I find myself saying the unthinkable out loud—"If it is your will"—passing on the decision to powers beyond us. But in that gesture of releasing him, I felt Rafaelito move toward us, toward life. Forty-five minutes into a three-and-a-half-hour surgery, Nurse Stacey comes in and tells us, "There was a small perforation in the intestine. The surgeons removed only two centimeters and the ileocecal valve. He's going to be fine."*

Soon after, my comadre Deborah arrives, "packed for survival." She creates an altar on the small lamp table from the holy cards and healing stones she has brought. We don't light the incense, but place the sage next to the burning candle enflaming the face of la Virgen. My rebozo becomes the altar cloth. We give thanks. Estér and Renée show up later. Ella has called them. "We need some family with us," she said. When Rafaelito is brought back to the ICN, he is a limp yellow doll, a stripped monkey naked under the glare of heat lamps. He is all wound, and he is my son, breathing through a respirator, stable, and so morphined he is feeling no pain. We finally get ourselves out of there.

Tede stays with our child, like an angel.

---

*Rather than reconnecting the intestine where the removal of the dead matter took place, the surgeons give the baby a temporary ileostomy in order to relieve stress on the colon. For the next three months, Rafaelito would be passing stool into a small bag attached to his lower right abdomen.

25 julio

For the first time since Rafaelito's transport to San Francisco, I've taken the day off, feeling a sore throat coming on. I call the nurse on duty. The news is good. All signs promising that Rafael is recovering well. I think of nothing, no one, but my baby, even as I wash the rugs, dry the dishes. Oh yes, surely as I pump my breasts, I imagine his miniature mouth opening onto the dark rose tip. I imagine the earliest most earnest seeking. I imagine his return to la madre from whom he was so abruptly separated, me, my womb, that sweet protection. The world outside, full of danger.

It is hard to write when there is no fixed me to be. I am not the same. I don't know how to write of death. I read The Tibetan Book of Living and Dying *and know I am like the majority, afraid to even name death, that somehow in the naming it will surely visit me. And yet I also know that this is the next necessary step. Rafaelito's close encounter with death, his tenuous hold on life, his fragile and threatened beginnings, have introduced me to living with the knowledge of death.*

26 julio

My baby's lungs are the size of teardrops, and I am still too afraid to fully cry.

Is it residual fear, now that my son heals himself, that causes the fire of an unnamed panic to rise up my spine, spilling across the back of my shoulders, flooding my heart, closing down my throat without warning? Daily we have watched fear's venom pass through plastic tubes, in and out of open veins and miniature organs. I know fear's scent pressed into the industrial detergent smell of my baby's doll-sized sheets and blankets. We carry its odorless indifference home with us on our clothes, in our skin. Susto, es susto.

The oxygen tube will be removed this morning. I pray for Rafaelito's strong lungs.

29 julio

Tonight I am unable to sleep. I get up, disturbed by what seems to be again an infection in my system, warding off a sore throat all week. I have felt off-balance for months now, since the advent of allergy season. "No one responded," I tell Ella. Throughout the last months of pregnancy, no one took my allergies, my sinus infections seriously. Yet a part of me feels that these infections are what wore me down, eventually causing the rupture of my membrane, the water breaking. We'll never know for sure.

1 agosto

Again last night we watched Rafaelito's energy wane, watched him recede into his miniature cuerpecito, lie low and await his own renewal: the transfusion of blood, the rush of antibiotics. This morning I call about his condition and revel in the news of his orneriness, his anger at not being fed. "He's kicking up a storm," Nurse Bobbie tells me. "He's mad we're not feeding him yet." A few hours later, we learn Rafa is eating—barely three cc's every two hours. He is on his own steam. And again I know my baby will pass through this, regain his health, return to us whole.

It is a return. His early separation was so radical, the wound of which is salved only in the sudden appearance of a droplet of milk at the lip of my tit, the movement of Rafael kicking against my belly as I hold him naked against the skin of my chest. His smell. His smell that grew sweet with the rise of milk inside my breasts, that grew sweet with woman-sex. Even my sister tells me, "I love that smell. I'll never forget that smell," knowing it four times in her life. She didn't mean some baby wrapped in the newborn warmth of a receiving blanket. She meant birth-smell, the thick-membraned blood-smell passing out between a woman's legs at birth and for a full moon's cycle following. I didn't tell her how close the scent came to that lesbian secret, of how close women come to birth each time we make love to one another and mean it. It is a lesbian sex-smell. A mother-smell. A mother-lover, a mother-fucked smell. It is life.

My baby's newborn smell sleeps in every item of tiny clothing—T-shirt, sleeper, knitted cap and booties—I lay out, fold and shape, and prepare for his arrival. The smell holds an innocence like nothing I imagined, only remembered vaguely in my own once-innocence. Ironically, as my baby grows older, he grows more innocent. He becomes more "baby" and less sabio, less viejito, less my mother's aging face and, instead, the seamless face of hopefulness, of future. But his hands retain the memory. Wrinkled, a map of generations revisited.

8 agosto

I saw God in him, in the simple act of will not to die. Like he had the power to choose. Only God got that power, I thought, until that moment. He was young enough, small enough to remember where he'd come from. He could've chosen to return.

Rafael is my poem. El milagro of what has passed and what will go forward. He is history and future as Tede now knows, as Audre was given the daily glimpse of for fifteen years, battling cancer. Through Rafael I have been given the gift of bearing witness to a soul's decision to take hold of an earthly life. We have stood on this side calling to him, "Come join us, hijo. Stay here with us." This time, we know he is going nowhere but into our arms, into the embrace of this worldly existence. He has made a decision that at twenty-eight weeks we didn't know for sure he would make. Now after five weeks on this planet, we know he will remain with us and "live to be a very old man," as Nurse Rose tells us.

Rose has become our "seer" of sorts, bringing in the holy cards of archangels and St. Jude, the "Patron of Lost Causes," as well as directives from her recently passed mother, who, according to Rose, was la mera Croatian curandera in Kansas City. Rose convinces me to make the trip over to the shrine of St. Jude, a mile or so from Kaiser at St. Dominic's Church. The edifice is a massive monument to San Francisco's Catholic elite, but inside I draw comfort from the stale scent of frankincense and the wintry childhood smell of melting votives. I follow Rose's directions and make my way up the side aisle to the shrine of St. Jude, ablaze with white candles. I slip a five into the metal slot, light five candles, and with each I pray not only for Rafa, but for all the babies and their ailments I've come to know in the ICN: for Alex, that her sleeping limbs will awaken; for Nathaniel, that his heart will heal; for Simone, that her eyes will see clear and far; for Freddy with Downs; and for all the others I've seen, mirroring Rafa's own embattled state—one- and two- and three-pound human animals with swollen brains and strokes and weak hearts and drug addictions and troubled families—just struggling to hold onto the little life they got.

Leaving the church, I run into a man asking for change and a prayer. For some reason, I tell him that my son is sick and in the hospital. He says he had a son once. I give him a twenty. I couldn't help it. I give him a twenty to ward off death.

15 agosto

Over six weeks in the hospital since Rafael Angel's birth. Six weeks. And we may have as much as another six weeks ahead of us. Ella and I are beginning to feel the aftershocks of our near-loss of Rafa. The last four days he struggles against a new infection, a staph infection, brought on by the IV needle implanted in his chest. We worry over what could still come in the months ahead.

I think of little else but him. Ella tells me I'm obsessed, but I know there is no other response to have. We wear each other down. I hear her cry, but I cannot comfort her. I move about as a nervous child. Fear—its violent rush of adrenaline—grows horribly familiar, and I clean and hammer and fill empty boxes and move furniture and do laundry and wash dishes and dishes with a vengeance against whom? Against death? Against its residual poison left in my bloodstream? I drown the taste out with a shot of tequila. I sleep a dreamless dead sleep to fortify myself for the next day.

It was harder than ever to leave Rafael in the hospital yesterday, to be parted from him. Each leave-taking a violent rupture. I return home without my child. Again empty-handed. Ella and I fight because we are tired and worried, and empty-handed. All is an effort, except the spontaneous impulse toward this baby. I am not inside this writing at all in my heart. I am across the city, my face pressed to the steaming plastic glass of Rafaelito's isolette.

17 agosto

Some change has taken place. The garden flourishes, although Ella battles daily against the onslaught of ants and aphids. Yesterday Rafael Angel looked better than ever, contento, tranquilo. Well-fed, his color took on a richness I hadn't seen since his birth. I put him to my breast, and he lives complete as a life's lesson in the moment of that suck-and-pull-and-rush of liquid filling his mouth and throat, settling full and sweet at the base of his hunger. His hunger, for now, can be satisfied.

21 agosto

I awake at 4:30 A.M. from a dream in which Rafael is suddenly losing weight. He is down to six hundred grams. He won't make it. I am beyond shock, beyond fear. Bobbie is the nurse in charge. She is not alarmed, only acquiescent in a way to his dying. I can't bear it. No one seems to be responding. He is slipping away. The feeling is strangely familiar, one that I had feared so much, lying dormant inside me throughout all these weeks since his birth—a sense of the inevitable finally coming to pass.

Writing at this hour (5:15 A.M.), I visualize Rafael Angel in his isolette in the hospital. I wonder if he is awake now. I realize as he energetically gains weight that with each gram he moves closer to his return to me, to us, to his home. I wonder if this morning's dream is larger than I think. With each gram, he also grows less and less dependent, less mine. He will never be mine and will surely pass away one day, as inevitably as my dream predicts it. And I am already parted from this body.

My parents are here to visit. A good visit. Much kindness. They seem quite content. I relish my time with them, the regularity of our meals together: the caldo we eat in the late afternoon, their midnight chicken sandwiches, my father's ritual glass of red wine. The gift of this child is how he has opened my eyes. I see my mother's amazing physical beauty, the quality of her skin, still sensual, seamless (the skin of a fifty-year-old at seventy-eight). She dresses in front of me, stands bare-breasted without shame. Is it motherhood that has made our bodies finally shameless to each other?

26 agosto

In the dream I am on the shore of the mainland. There is an island out in the water. Tidal waves ravage it as hundreds of people rush to the mainland for safety. The tidal waves are huge. I am awed by their grandeur. The people that rush to shore are beach-goer types: white people, young, moneyed. Suddenly I realize my parents are on the island. I worry that they have been consumed by the storm. Then my father appears from out of the water. He is dressed in white. His calm is almost christ-like as he surfaces. He walks toward the shore without fear. I wonder about my mother when suddenly she, too, appears, but her safety is threatened. There are tidal waves surrounding her. I hear a voice. It is the voice of Ella or my sister. It tells me to go in there and save my mother. I am shocked that this has not occurred to me. I know I cannot save her, that it would be a false gesture, that I would surely drown, but the voice insists that I go in there. I awaken.

10 septiembre

I could have held him for two hours in the darkness of that nursing room, in the silence, simulating that place from where he emerged, not violently but of his own volition. But there was the fear of falling asleep while holding him bundled as he was, the fear of him falling too deeply into my arms where his breath might not find release, fear of suffocation. This is a mother's fear, I know, a mother's guilt as I bring him back into the hospital nursery. The nurse reminds me, "Probably the first time since his birth he had things so quiet." Can I ever make it up to him, those last three months in the womb lost? Then I imagine the endless hours when he will have both silence and darkness and also the warm embrace of my breast...when I get him...when I get him home.

25 septiembre

Endless hours still yet to come in the ICN, watching our baby move from isolette to crib, from two to three to four pounds. Endless hours yet to come before I can get Rafaelito home. Two full weeks pass without crisis. Today is my birthday.

Returning from the ocean, I call the hospital, speak with Nurse Rose. She tells me Rafaelito has made me a birthday card. She tells me the story of getting his spindly legs to stay put onto the ink. His signature, a footprint in a card. Earlier today I came into the ICN, and Ella had arranged for a cake to be awaiting me, again signed by Rafaelito.

"Felíz cumpleaños, Mamá," it said, and I still marvel at the miracle that someone will soon grow to call me mami.

Ella and I walk the beach. It is all I really wanted to do for my birthday, to meditate on the glass wall of wave that crashes onto the shoreline. Sandpipers scurry along the wet sand, burrow their beaks in search of sand crabs. I remember my own childhood. How, like the sandpipers, I learned to read the signs of where the crabs were buried, bubbles of air cracking the smooth surface of the sand, their soft-shelled bodies hidden less than an inch below. I am too exhausted to write tonight, but I only wanted to record my bottomless joy at the entrance of Rafael into my life, of the ever-awe of what was not present with me, suddenly appearing and residing in my heart.

28 septiembre

I try to dissect the wild scrawl. Ronnie's* handwriting. He speaks of his imminent death. Although in good health, he says he considers it constantly since learning he is positive. He asks me not to write of him posthumously. "No obituaries," he says, as were done for Tede. He wants only to be remembered by his poems, as we all wish, to be remembered for our poems.

But I have forgotten how to write the poem, the play. I read Ronnie's letter where he mentions at least five writers I do not know, but Bob Kaufman—the Black Beat poet, now gone—was not one of the unknown to me, and I dream of doing nothing other than reading until I know them all, until I have something to write again.

These days I feel I never fully inhabit the hours. Even while watching Rafael's small, sculpted "African head," as Myrtha calls it, as he sucks my breast, I feel that I am missing him. I don't realize my utter frustration at the length of his hospital stay, now going into the fourth month.

---

*Ronnie Burk, Chicano poet, prophet, and visual artist.

I don't fully absorb the recent news that there may yet be another blockage in his intestine, another cut-and-paste job on the operating table on Friday, instead of what was to have been a "routine operation."* I don't know the depth of my own anger until I hear myself raging on Deborah's answering machine. "There is nothing to fear but fear itself," I shout, "and it is consuming me!" I cling to Rafaelito, hold my ears against bad news. I am that stricture, that blockage between him and all that threatens him.

I grow weary of the low-level fear running concurrently with my life, that always around the corner there will be another problem the doctors failed to mention. I worry over how much intestine will be lost, over the pain Rafaelito will experience. I worry that he must go hungry for days without my milk to sustain him.

3 octubre/ICN

Second day after Rafaelito's surgery. To our relief, no more intestine was lost. "A simple procedure," the doctors told us, simply reconnect the small and large intestine, sew up the stoma. Two days later, Ella holds Rafa in her arms with a respirator down into his lungs, two IV's stuck into the veins in his head, and a tube running down his throat to suck out leakage in his stomach. He has dehydrated, is unable to urinate. And my baby has bloated up to twice his body-size. His face is a monster's—his eyes, black seeds buried into a mass of fluid. When I put my hand to his cheek to caress him, the imprint remains, deforming him.

We learn later that during his pre-op preparation, the nurses (as instructed by the surgeon) had overcleaned the intestines. I had seen the colon cleanser going through him like Drano. The kid was dehydrating before the operation, and his kidneys eventually

---

*The surgery was to re-open the first incision from the ileostomy, close up the stoma, and reconnect the intestine so that Rafael could once again pass stool normally.

stopped functioning. I am more worried when the surgeon comes to see him. Dr. Azick wears wide-ribbed corduroy pants. It is the weekend; he doesn't have to be here, so he must be worried, too. And then he admits it. "Frankly, I'm concerned. I don't know what's wrong." I appreciate the admission, but don't like what follows: "If his condition doesn't change soon, we'll have to go in again."

Ella and I come back for a second visit that same day. After 8:00 P.M. we must enter through the emergency entrance, where a security guard gives us passes after signing us in. The guard laboriously tries to spell out my name, letter by letter. The pen is a stranger to him, and I feel my impatience rise, as does my anxiety about Rafaelito. I just want to get in there and see my baby. But each night we go through the same interrogation. "Only immediate family," the young man tells us. He is very serious in his fresh-pressed uniform. He is taking his job very seriously. "Yes, we know," I answer for the hundredth time. "She (referring to Ella) is immediate family. Call the ICN. They'll okay us." The same old ritual, the same harassment night after night. Then he can't help himself, and a grin begins to crack the professional facade. "You say you're both the moms!" He eyes his buddies, his co-workers, and the street gang begins to form around us. Oh, they're gonna milk this one for all its worth. They are very bored. "I didn't know two women could have a baby together."

But I am primed, too. Thinking of Rafaelito swollen beyond recognition. *Don't fuck with me tonight, boys.* We had already filed our complaints over earlier harassment, called their supervisor who always seemed to enjoy the joke as much as they did, spoken with the ICN social worker, and in a few days I would write the obligatory letter to the hospital administrator. Pero, para nada. Nobody really gives a damn that two women have their baby in a hospital for over three months, not knowing if he is going to live or die, and they still have to endure insults from testosterone-driven homophobes with no power acting like they got some. (My class and race analysis don't do shit for me when the brothers are standing in the way of my child. The hospital was full of AIDS patients, and Ella and I often wondered how *their* lovers were treated when they came through the same door after-hours.)

That night I can't take any more. All I can see is Rafael's tiny face buried inside that mask of bloated flesh. "That's right," I answer, "you'd be surprised what two women can do together." And I storm through the entrance cursing and screaming at the top of my lungs, hoping Ella's coming up behind me. The guard is shouting after me, but I don't hear anything beyond "Hey, lady..." I am counting in my mind how many times we've gone through this, how many times Ella has had to succumb to questioning when she's called the ICN and a new receptionist answers. "Who are you? What is your relationship to Rafael Moraga?" It's been over three months, for chrissakes! My impotence enrages me. I can't protect her from the pain she experiences each time they make her the outlaw. I'm the dyke in the matter, I tell myself. I'm the one who's supposed to be on the outside. But not now. As Rafael's biological mother, I am surrounded by acceptance at the hospital, until Ella walks in and we are again the lesbian couple, the queer moms— exoticized or ostracized. I know this is new for Ella. New and hard. As a femme, she's always passed effortlessly, that is, until she opens her mouth and the lesbian feminist spills forth without restraint.

If anyone had stopped me that night at the emergency entrance, I'm sure I would have belted him. Fortunately, no one does, and minutes later Ella joins me at the elevator. We ride up to the third floor in silence.

4 octubre

I sit at the edge of a San Francisco fishing pier. It is minutes after dawn. This morning, the fog prevents any dramatic sunrise from behind the Oakland hills, but as the ashy light gradually turns the bay waters from black to green-grey, there is renewed hope. I come to this pier today looking for hope, as I did nine months ago, having just heard the news of my pregnancy. It was a winter night, and I carried the seed of who I did not know then was Rafaelito to the pier's end. Together we floated out into the obsidian waters, harbor lights swimming inside them. We drifted under the Golden Gate and out into the Pacific sea in my dream of the future we would share. There was no doubt then (as there isn't now, learning this morning that Rafa was breathing on his own) that that future would come to pass. But there certainly has been doubt since that time, core doubt, or more accurately, a deadening fear.

A woman, middle-aged like me, interrupts this writing, asks can she take my picture. She looks familiar to me. "It's a class assignment," she says. I respond, "I don't care." And I don't, for she has a kind smile and is a simple woman, as I am.

I walk the pier in search of the simple, the daily miracles of which my son's relentless struggle to be here reminds me. The pier houses the homeless overnight. It is a stupid term for people, but that's what I call them in my mind as I pass the makeshift tents, the shopping carts pinned against royal blue plastic tarp to keep out the wind. Now a tugboat passes by, otro milagro perfectly red-and-white striped, perfectly tugboat, steadily churning its way under the Bay Bridge. The bridge is the same color as the sky, steel grey. The cars travel across it, miniature in the distance, and everything becomes my baby's point of reference: the tugboat story in children's books, Tonka trucks, miniature cars that my (almost) son used to horde and collect by the dozens.

The day has entered fully into itself now, as I hope Rafaelito will when I go to visit him this morning under the heat of warming lamps and a web of IVs. I pass joggers in sweatpants on my way back, thick-waisted centro americanos in nylon windbreakers, una latina lifting her knees to her chin military-marching style. Her morning exercises. The gulls continue to hover in anticipation of fishermen. In hours their bellies will be full of fish gut and discarded pieces of bagel. The ferries are in full steam, commuting before my eyes' horizon with ten-minute regu-

larity. I, too, pull away from the docks and make my way toward my regular morning commute: Kaiser Hospital, San Francisco.

5 octubre

The next several days are to be the last leg of this journey. Suddenly I grow afraid of how dependent we have become on the women who have nursed Rafa through these three months: Rose, Stacey, Bobbie, Sue, Gurline, Donna, Terry, and others whom we never met who watched him throughout the night while we slept or tried to sleep.

Three months. Hard to imagine such a length of time, even in retrospect. But it is not our dependence on the nurses that I fear, so much as the loss of the connection. These women have become our family, the only ones who have known intimately, on a daily level, the heartache we endure. I know some of them have even come to love Rafa, thinking of him as "their baby," and getting some serious attitude when he's not listed as one of theirs for the shift. Seeing them fight over Rafael tells me how attached they've become to him, and maybe, without admitting it, they've even become a little attached to us. With no man in the way, Ella and I have sat with these women 'til eleven on Saturday nights, shooting the shit about their love lives—their crazy jazz musician boyfriends and soon-to-be marriages in the midst of a Yugoslavian civil war. We've befriended the one dyke couple in the nursery, after it took me nearly two months to figure it out. We've talked politics, sex, fashion (at least Ella has), and "alternative lifestyles." One time Ella even suggested to one of the more butchy-looking nurses, who was quite a wild woman with the men, that she might want to try women for a change. Well, I guess that was going a little too far. She iced Ella for a full month after that.

Although I am ever-grateful to Dr. Azick, the soft-spoken pediatric surgeon from UCSF who saved my baby's life on that operating table, the nurses have been the real healers. We've counted on them to remember how Rafael looked the day before, to notice when his color has paled or energy waned, to respond to signals in advance when his oxygen saturation level dropped or he wasn't keeping down his food. They have advocated for him when the doctors weren't listening. They are the ones who, around the clock, have tended to my son with a woman's love, a mother's love, who have made the difference, fundamentally, in his survival.

6 octubre

My baby has returned home to us in the dream. He is extremely vulnerable. At a theater event, I show him to my friends. He is a small worm, the color of the stoma that used to protrude from the side of his belly, a deep pinkish red. His face is a design of small markings, like brush strokes. There are no real features. I accept his appearance as perfectly normal. My friend queries, "He will grow, won't he?"

Other dreams follow the same pattern. He is so tiny, so vulnerable. I sometimes forget that I have him, start to leave a place without him. At other times Ella forgets him. He is always on the verge of disappearing, melting away, dissolving in water.

8 octubre

Today, this day, may be the one of Rafaelito's return to us after all. It has been an everyday occurrence since Friday—the promise of his coming home, followed by the disappointment. Yet, I feel the time closing in; it could surely be today. The grey dawn invites his coming. I check the date. He is a Libra baby of sorts, entering the "outside" world about ten days after his original due date. All this time he was to have been growing in my womb. Instead he is rushed into this world and has survived a two-pound-six-ounce birth weight, two major surgeries, and myriad infections.

We have an enormous amount to be grateful for—fundamentally his life. That he was born in 1993, not 1963, and there were surgeons to find and root out his illnesses early on. But more importantly, that from the beginning of his life he was surrounded by great love. Yes, the love from his caregivers, the nurses who came to feel Rafaelito was a part of them. But also, the love from my blood familia and all my queer relations, with candles burning across the continent toward his survival.

Throughout the wee hours of the morning, the U.S. Air Force's Blue Angels strip the sky of its necessary quiet. Ironic, I think, their name— my son's name—his innocence and vulnerability against their steel delight in stripping off the canopy of our heavenly protection. Angels, they are not. It is too early to be awake, and yet I know my baby will have me up at this hour most days. I look forward to those moments of solitude with him. His crib and cradle and changing table are cov- ered with cloths—as during Lent, I can't help thinking, awaiting the resurrection. All is in order.

16 octubre

Rafael Angel is discharged from the hospital.

It is a full week later than expected, always some unexpected "compli- cation" or "potential problem" cropping up. The nurses kept reassur- ing, "It's better this way. The worse thing is to get him home and to have to bring him back again." Unfathomable, I think.

Nurse Bobbie, fittingly, is the one to do the honors. We marvel at how everything comes full circle, her picking Rafaelito up in Los Angeles, admitting him in San Francisco. Now three and a half months later, she does the paperwork for his discharge, and we load up to get this kid home. And I mean *load up:* the cards, the stuffed animals, the mobiles, the little notes Nurse Rose made in her curled calligraphy, the angel figures of every shade and shape, the tiny wardrobe of T-shirts and sleepers, doll-sized knit caps and booties, the handmade blanket from my Tía Eva, the photographs of Rafa at various stages in his hospital stay (some with his little ICN neighbors held up by moms and nurses grinning in the background), the thumb-sized moccasins Cynthia and Dina brought from Pine Ridge, Deborah's healing stones and Stacey's arrowheads, the stone angel my sister gave him on her visit here, Angelina's tiny indio doll, and finally, the green-and-white felt-covered image of la Virgen my mother had given me when I first went into the hospital over fifteen weeks earlier. I had pasted the scapular to Rafael's incubator in Hollywood on his birthday. It remained with him through the trip up north, into the operating room, and throughout his entire stay at Kaiser, San Francisco.

We pile all of this—what had decorated Rafaelito's "apartment" (the nurses' name for his crib)—onto a wheelchair, along with a bag full of medicine, complimentary diapers and formula, and a preemie-sized bathing tub (Rafa is still under five pounds). After last-minute pictures with nurses and docs, Ella carries Rafa's carseat, I carry Rafa, and Bobbie maneuvers the wheelchair/moving van out of the ICN. As the elevator opens onto the lobby floor, Ella and I spot two dyke moms coming in with their baby. The first and only lesbian moms we've seen in almost four months. And this is San Francisco.

Later, stuffed into the front seat of my little truck, Ella and I keep eyeing the sleeping bundle next to us. Free at last, I know we're both thinking. No cliché. *Free at last.*

III
Dream of a Desert

Babies change things,
open doors you thought were shut,
close others.
Make you into something you never been.
You the mama now,
you're gonna think different.

Dorothy Allison,
Two or Three Things I Know for Sure

1. The Face of Change

The first year of our life together

It is a series of moments that are the mundane world of sleepless nights, ear infections, and petty arguments. It is hallmarked by the ordinary: baby rolling over, baby sitting up, baby crawling, baby taking his first step.* It is the indoor world of domestic bliss and blame, the delicacy of sentiment and solidity of faithfulness. It is a world that begins and ends at home.

The first year of our life together is seldom recorded in daily journals. My work and its requirements return: the teaching jobs, speaking gigs, the play commissions. Not nine-to-five, but nine-to-nine or six o'clock in the morning to midnight or 3:00 A.M. or any time the time can be squeezed in to do the writing, create a livelihood, a life's work.

The first years of our life together are a series of small movements, epiphanies, changes. They are the road taken toward life...and death, those deaths that witness my baby in the beginning of his life. When my baby was born, he was born with history. And as we bury our loved ones, history continues. It is that endless circle of birth/death/rebirth that we Mexicans have always bemoaned and celebrated, dancing drunk with life around the lip of the grave.

I try to teach Rafael Angel "hide & seek." I throw a cloth over a small blue plastic block. He realizes it has vanished. It appears that he understands, for the first time, that the block may be underneath the cloth—if he were to take a look. But those are too many ifs to bother with right now. I can see him thinking this as his almond eyes roll over, ever so subtly, to another toy clearly visible and attainable. He

---

*Ordinary, but in the case of Rafael, never taken for granted. Each of these "normal" stages of development occurred three to six months "late" for Rafa, but gratefully, always did occur.

goes for it, springing onto it like a young cub. And I begin to laugh, the deepest laugh, the richest of familial laughs. I bring Rafa into my arms, and every cell of my body is filled with joy at his entrance into this world, his developing and discriminating mind, his pure presence. I laugh so hard I cry, and wet his face with my tears, my kisses, my hope in the face of death.

2 noviembre/Día de los Muertos

I feel something has broken in me, and yet I am forced to proceed along as if everything were normal. I am a mother now and I do not yet know how to fully inhabit that place in the world. In the small confines of my home, with Ella, with my familia, there is a sense of rightness, but nowhere else. That susto that took hold of me for so long isn't so easily exorcised. Everything is changed. My writer's heart feels stolen by the struggle for my baby's survival.

Those last weeks in the hospital, we waited each day to see that Rafaelito was assimilating his food properly. There had been diarrhea, blood in the stool. We waited. Now I wonder how long to wait for a cry to stop, what his cries mean. I am awake before and through the dawn while the rest of the house sleeps. There is a restlessness in me, not due to lack of sleep, but lack of confidence. I miss the immersion into my writing terribly, fear I will not be able to resurrect that impassioned momentum. The baby cries.

Sleep deprivation. I remember my comadres warning me of this physical state, near-madness. Rafael was used to round-the-clock daylight in the Intensive Care Nursery. Darkness does not mean sleep to him. He awakens three or four times a night.

One night at 2:30 A.M. I break down, move out of the bed with Ella and into Rafael Angel's room. I throw the futon on the floor, cover it with flannel sheets and the down comforter, stick the kid inside, and we sleep like odd-sized twins together. I throw him the tit at his every stirring, and he falls out again. Adding up the hours this way, I get more sleep than waiting for his squeal from the next room, feeding him, then coaxing him back to sleep for two hours. Ella definitely gets more sleep. I worry, what does this mean? The child has moved my woman and me into separate beds. But I assure myself it is a temporary arrangement.

Of course, there are those moments of peace. Getting in the bath with Rafa, I see his body relax in a way I imagine it hasn't since utero. Floating, floating. His fists unclench, his arms fall back to the sides of his head, his chest receives the water. Yes, a baby seal, his sweet slick skin, that sense of belonging. I almost detect a smile. "The book" says Rafaelito should be smiling by now, by his "adjusted age."* Still, there is no clearly convinced smile, only an impressive, intelligent frown. I hate baby books. I only turn to them to make sure I am making no grave errors. I resent these white male pediatrician-types with their nurse-wives and seven kids "bonding" their way into my Mexican psyche. Rafael was born with a seriousness about him. It was the place of strength he drew from to fight the diseases that plagued him at birth. His smiles will come.

8 diciembre

I sneak out my journal for twenty minutes of writing (if I'm lucky) before Rafaelito rises with his morning cry. Some days are more difficult than others. Some days Rafael Angel is a non-stop complaint from seven in the morning 'til midnight. Ella refutes it, but I know it is when we start the day arguing. About time schedules. About time. I know he senses something "off," even though I hold him as I cry and

---

*A premature baby's adjusted age is determined by his/her due date (or the date on which they actually leave the hospital) rather than the premature birthdate. Therefore, for the first two years, Rafael's development will be measured according to his "adjusted age," i.e. three-and-a-half months younger than his actual age. Usually by the third year, a preemie's development has caught up with his/her age.

repeat over and over again, *"Esto no tiene nada que ver contigo, hijo."* I can't rid myself of the knowledge of how young I was when I felt my mother's unhappiness. *"At her breast,"* a psychic once told me, and her words come as no surprise.

Ella spent an hour with me today, an hour she didn't have, giving me the courage to continue with my work. At the lowest point in my physical stamina, I fall into despair about my writing. The baby cries...again. I want to smother a slowly surfacing guilt that my concern has shifted from baby to work so suddenly. Less than two months ago, I worried for his life. I still worry, only the anxiety has abated somewhat. And in the lessening of the fear, there is a small aperture, a glimmer of a longing to create again. Oh, it's a luxury to be sure, reserved for the well-fed and healthy (when Rafa's life was threatened, I couldn't write a line); but now, coming out from under the sea of that terror, I need the work, the writing, more passionately than ever. I need to know I am more than these tasks of motherhood, more than mother. I need to remember that I am a writer.

12 diciembre/Día de Guadalupe

This is my first visit with my son to the Sacred Tree in Watsonville. I have come with Pablo and our friend Ricky to fulfill la promesa y dar gracias a la Virgen de los Cannery Workers for saving my baby's life.* I especially have a need to ask for forgiveness, for paciencia, for open-heartedness. There has been a relentless rigidity in me since the baby's birth, more so since his return home. I maintain a furious order in the house and Ella often complains of it, feeling a stranger in her own home.

Rafaelito is so tiny I can wrap him up in my rebozo and nurse him, unnoticed under the shelter of the oaks. I nurse and rock, nurse and

---

*In 1992, the image of La Virgen de Guadalupe was spotted on an old oak tree in the Mexican-Californian town of Watsonville. Pilgrims visit the site with supplications.

rock, as the women sing oraciones a la Virgen in that flat Mexican key de las viejitas. Pablo and Ricky stand in the outer circle of prayer. There all the men are gathered. Vaquero hats in their hands, their black hair glistens in the sunlight.

It is difficult to see through the crowd of women surrounding the tree, but I spot the head of a woman (a mother) bent over her child who has been brought before la Virgen's image. The child is about six or seven, sitting in a tall stroller. I had noticed him as we first arrived, his long legs hanging down from the high seat. (Too old for a stroller, I think.) I didn't realize he was unable to walk until now as the mother pulls the boy up, grabbing him under the arms. A small group of mujeres encircle him. La jefa, a woman in her seventies, a thick rope of grey braid going down her back, holds her hands over the boy's head, asking for the Virgen's intercession. Help the boy walk is the prayer. Let the boy walk. The mother and the other women pull the child around on spaghetti legs. He's loving it, being the center of attention, bobbing about in front of the crowd. He wears a sweet payaso grin on his face. I wish to God the kid would get up and walk, too, but hate seeing them put him through it. The hope. Maybe he is too young to hope like we do. Maybe he is just having a good time. But the mother isn't. Crying up a storm when the boy doesn't walk, probably knowing he isn't going to. Hoping against hope. And I am there in that mother's skin, as I pull Rafaelito into me, holding on for his dear life, his dear health. Knowing I could've been her. Still can.

Sometimes I fear what would happen should Rafael ever get seriously ill again. My memory of his near-death is so close to me, still so visceral in my gut. At times, when Rafaelito exhibits even the slightest sign of a cold, I feel that sudden rush of adrenaline, that panic. I fear he will not survive. I know the fear is not logical, that it emerges from that region where I carry the memory of his two-pound spirit being rolled down the hospital corridor on his way to surgery. Those same deep dark eyes looking up at me as if to reassure me he would indeed survive. I am afraid of loving this much, afraid to be so vulnerable to the fragile life of another human being. Take my life instead, I can say without hesitation.

Later that night

I sit at the side of my baby's cradle and gradually rock him to sleep. It is always something of a miracle that I can coax him to sleep without trickery, just putting him down, well-fed, him drifting off into slumber. I watch the slow rise and fall of his chest. There is always a subtle rocking to his body as he sleeps, the same rocking I remember we discovered in the ICN. Each time Rafaelito was released from the cradle of our arms and returned to his isolette, he would continue the movement, the ritmo, the motion of comfort, of cariño, of continuance.

In honor of la Virgen's feast day, Pablo has given Rafaelito his first "picture book." (That's what Pablo called it.) An Uncertain Grace, *photographs by Brazilian Sebastiao Salgado. I am struck by an image I spy over Ella's shoulder as she flips the pages. An African woman supports the bodies of two starving babies as they each suck from her breasts. The breasts sag aged and milkless into their mouths. At first all I see is the horror de la hambre. Then I look more deeply and notice the delicate vein running along the woman's arm, the grace and beauty of those babies' proud chests, muscular limbs, the strength and desire for life in those fists that grab at the woman's breasts. The twins are my son, his pathetic thinness at birth, his clinging animal heart and hunger.*

The woman remains faceless, but I know how she looks. I know her infinite fatigue, the futility of a suck that can draw no sweet succor, no sustenance. She feels herself an empty woman. Her breasts, brown barren sacks of crumpled paper, such thirsty breasts. One baby, with the fine hard African skull, wears a beaded necklace. Against all odds for his survival, this baby's entrance into the world is decorated. These twins are my baby's cousins. They are survivors.

In an inscription in the book, Pablo wrote to Rafael: "Para su primer día de Lupita, que nuestra belleza, lucha y cultura siempre te llene." There was a rush of emotion reading the words, a resonance, an echo I felt, a longing met. Those are the words that keep me from saying so freely to Ella, yes, should I pass on, the baby goes to you alone, unequivocally. Es la cultura.

There is no denying that I had this baby that he might be a Mexican, for him to know and learn of mexicanismo, for him to feel that fuego, that llama, that riqueza I call lo mexicano. And for a moment, I miss that Mexican loving in my life.

I know this is the "half-breed" in me speaking, she who stands at the generational crossroads of a family. She who bears witness as the Mexican vanishes into the generation that precedes her. She who wants to "not vanish" as a people...as a person.

I dream that night that my friends, Inés and Cathy, and I are part of a danza group. In conversation with one of the male leaders, a sloppily dressed macho, Inés complains to him that there are no babies present. He brings her another woman's child to appease her. She is not pleased. She is worried that it is separated from its mother. We dance in a circle. Inés gives Cathy a unique kind of tambor with two bowl-like parts; one part has a kind of paddle with which to drum. Inés gives me only the one piece without the paddle. I am disappointed because I want to learn to play the tambor. But as we dance, she begins to instruct me—half-piece that I am.

Nochebuena/San Gabriel

Only before dawn can I find the silence, the solitude, to write here in the home of my youth. It is strangely ironic that my baby of nearly six months sleeps peacefully in the bedroom that once enclosed my tormented adolescent dreams of desire. The same desire called him into

91

this planet and now roots him here among the family of his maternal grandmother's namesake: Moraga. Coming home will never be the same, coming home with this child. I now always will return a mother. Mother: the term assumes the shape of my being very gradually. Yesterday I hear the word fall from my sister's mouth as she plays with Rafaelito. I am, for a moment, taken aback when I realize that she is not referring to our mother, but is speaking to my son of me. We laugh at my still-virgin response. The intellect not quite caught up to biology.

It is now early morning, and my baby swings idly in an electric contraption meant just for such purposes. My mother warms the tortillas on the comal and my dad finishes off breakfast. Rafael is content, lulled by the steady rhythm of the automatic swing and still within watchful eye of his ever-growing familia. My mother sighs, "They grow up so fast." I know exactly what she means—that this baby swinging in the doorway is already somewhere in time a very old man, and I and my parents are long gone. There is a way that Rafael's arrival is an announcement of their own imminent passing. My parents wonder, I know, how much of his growing up they will be privileged to witness. "In good health," my mother adds. I wonder the same.

At times like these I want to split my mouth and throat wide open, drink in something so quickly vanishing in the daily growing up of nephews and nieces as breasts appear and voices change and Adam's apples suddenly emerge from adolescent male throats and hips continue to round in the bodies of little skinny girls turning into women. We record history as it passes from holiday to holiday, visit to visit, with a kind of tacit agreement that the photos and cards—the documentation—may have to suffice for my son as the reflection of an enormous love he may not consciously remember by the time he is fully grown. Life and death. Beginnings and endings. Spirits become flesh, then give up the ghost of the body.

Days ago, we visited the ghost of my grandmother. My Tío Bobby, Tía Eva, and parents encircle the gravesite. I wonder, as I place my son onto the rug of crew-cut lawn blanketing the spot, if these two did not already know each other. Could Rafael be the messenger boy of the now-dead matriarch? My tío speaks cariñosas to his "querida mamacita," as my mother and tía pick at some crabgrass scratching the edges of the tombstone. We fill a tin can with water, put a handful of garden roses into its mouth and into the mouth of the grave. We place a holiday poinsettia next to it. We pray the rosary like canto, my mother leading the prayer. This is how we remember Rafael's bisabuela for Christmas. This is how my family honors its dead.

Año Nuevo (1994)/Back in San Francisco

Since Rafaelito's entrance into this life with us, exhaustion dominates all other feelings. But Ella and I wait up anyway, as commanded by social law, to greet the new year in the still cold of this December San Francisco night. The longest nights of the year. Ella reads. Rafael sleeps. I write.

I write to remind myself on the eve of the new year that I am a writer, although I return from my ten-day stay in L.A. not quite convinced. I see Spielberg's new movie of the Jewish Holocaust and I am reminded of the human capacity for the most brutal and obscene cruelties. I question what I am worth, never having confronted that life-and-death choice between honor and survival. To sacrifice oneself for others is the most noble, the most human response; survival instinct, the most banal. For what is survival other than animal? I am an animal for my child. I knew that watching the mothers in the film, separated from their children, clawing like wild wounded lionesses.

I am too exhausted to write. Only want to ask—what am I doing about man's capacity for cruelty?

On that I end the year.

The Eve of the Equinox

So long since I have written here.

Yesterday, early morning, I awaken to the news that Myrtha's father has passed. Myrtha does not call me. Instead, I learn this from a friend with whom Myrtha had been living for a time. For Myrtha, the friend was a brief stopover en route to another life, the life after sixty, the life after the death of our parents, when we are nobody's child. Myrtha is my child, or at least I feel for her a mother's protectiveness, a mother's worry. Not that it is such sad news. A ninety-four-year-old man joins his wife barely a year after her passing. The good news is that Myrtha had brought him home from the hospital, that her son took the grandfather into his arms, bathed him, held him like a baby and rocked him into death. His final wish: to go from home to the grave. And so it was. I light a velador for Don Rafael and search for the medal of San Rafael that Nurse Rose had given me. I hang it over the head of the flame.

"What did the old man die of?" I ask Myrtha's friend.

"An obstruction in the intestine," she responds. "There was blockage where the small and large intestine meet." Her words chill me. "It's very serious."

"Yes," I answer. "I know."

And I wonder at the meaning of the news, that Don Rafael should die of the condition Rafaelito confronted three weeks after his birth, that I had named my son Rafael, never consciously knowing Myrtha's father's name, never knowing Rafaelito also carried the name of Myrtha's brother who had died in childhood. Spirits become flesh, then give up the ghost of the body...only to become flesh, again.

May Day

Change. I don't know the face of change.

> *"They say that snakes go blind for awhile before*
> *they shed their skin for the last time."*
>
> Toni Morrison, Jazz

Is it blind rage that spills out from me so utterly on the edge of despair, the edge of transformation? Am I blind to love, to real heartache in the eyes of my beloved, my Ella? I think of nothing but myself, my son. "There is nothing left over," I tell Ella. I remember the astrologer assuring me. "Forty-two," she said, "will mark the end of the seven-year cycle. A breakthrough of the old pattern," she predicted. "You will have resolved your relationships to such a degree that they will no longer serve as obstacles to your writing." But I feel no resolve. Not today.

I will never write the same. Maybe that is part of the metamorphosis the astrologer predicted. With the appearance of Rafael in my life, I can never return to the writer I once was. Not because of the time constraints, which are awesome, but because my soul is never completely empty in the same way. I am conscious of another entity always pulling on me. I don't know really how *Medea* emerged, even in the rough form she presently wears, but the writing did not feel the same. It did not take a piece of me in the same way earlier writing has. The writing isn't any less challenging, but now a hole has been created through which my child passed. (Don Juan speaks of this.) Now the work—the art—passes through me differently. I can't say how, exactly.

Rafaelito watches me write. He is not interested in the baby gym set dangling over his head. He is interested in the movement of my hand across this page. Black strokes against the soft beige grain of this paper. He watches me. And for the first time it occurs to me that he may have something to learn from me, by my example. "This is my work,

95

hijo. I am a writer." I am trying to be a mother who writes well. I am trying to be a writer who mothers well. Somewhere inside me, I feel the forces rise up to stop me.

Last night, I am lying on one end of the couch, listening to the arias of Maria Callas, Rafaelito asleep in my arms. Ella is stretched out on the other end, hand on my foot. I think about what it is to create—even for a single moment—a thing of beauty, a thing of pure and honest human passion, as these arias. I think of my own task as a writer—a life task—to write anything that comes close, even for a moment, to the depth of human emotion. At times I question it all. I wonder if I can ever truly create a complete work, something I can stand in the center of and know its wholeness.

Metamorphosis. Change. Tranformación.

Tonight is a sad night. After a typically fog-covered San Francisco morning, and a beautiful summerlike afternoon, this evening in this silent room seems sad. Is change sad? A letting go. I am afraid to look at how fundamentally Rafa's presence in our lives has changed Ella and me—each, her own life, and our life together. There is no return. Is it the past I mourn, that freedom? I scarcely remember her. Wonder of this new one. This me. This writer-mother. This often-troubled lover. The sage smoke brings a kind of calm, the smell comforting, cleansing. There is the need for quiet: reading into the late evening with Ella nearby, the baby resting peacefully.

Rafael's First Birthday/New York City

Ironically, I repeat the very journey I took last year, six months pregnant, feet and hands swelling in steaming subway stations, walking down 42nd Street each day toward the Hudson on my way to rehearsal, then finally joining Ella at the Cape to recover. I have returned to New York to see the Heart of the Earth *through its final phase of rehearsals for the world premiere. Rafa's Tía Cathy has come with me to care for Rafaelito while I work at the theater. Today is his birthday, and as it is the Fourth of July weekend, we have the day off to celebrate. We stuff Rafaelito into the stroller and make our way to Central Park, stopping here and there for party supplies: an ice chest of beer, a carrot cake, a loaf of french bread, cheese, a candle in the shape of the number one. Pablo and posse meet us in front of the Museum of Natural History across from the park. This colored queerboy contingent has been in New York for weeks now to celebrate the twenty-fifth anniversary of Stonewall. But they know they are not fully a part of those festivities, although it was their kind that started the rebellion a quarter of a century ago. They are not white nor monied nor just homo—they are colored boys. And in that sense, how glad I am to be in their company, to bring my son into their circle of fine and critical minds, smart mouths, and indignant dignity.*

We party. Pablo holds Rafaelito while Cathy tries to get him to blow out his candle. I snap the camera. To capture the time, to remember this picture of youth: elegant dark limbs stretched across the damp summer-green grass, their laughter. I felt that way once too, when New York was thoroughly contained in my lesbiancoloredgirl grasp. Rafael fidgets in Pablo's arms. We blow the candle out for him, and I make a wish like a prayer that my son will always have such men, such hope in his life.

4 julio

Maybe it is the motionless humidity of this city, maybe the sheer fact of the anniversary, that causes me to remember Rafaelito's sudden birth in a way I had never before. Something brings me back to that moment in time. San Gabriel. Hitting the bed just after breakfast, the water breaking open inside of me, and I feared my tiny baby had broken open, too. But he waited. Warrior that he is, he waited, and on the seventh day he came, on the seventh day of labor rooms, heart monitors, IVs, fear of infection. Flat on my back and praying, my baby came into this world. Born in Los Angeles, as the generation before him.

What is hardest to write about is the loss I feel not having brought Rafael to full term. At times I think it is loss, then wonder if it's really guilt I feel that my son had to go through so much suffering outside the womb because I couldn't protect him inside. There's no one to blame really, no matter how many times I run all the events through my mind.

I am standing on a subway train, my feet so swollen. And a young woman offers me her seat. In all my years of subway riding in New York City, no one had ever offered me a seat. I don't understand why the woman keeps gesturing to the seat she has just vacated for me, until I realize that she can see I am pregnant. I gracefully decline, determined as I am to balance my weight with the jostling of the train. I figure the baby finds the movement comforting, como una cuna rocking.

But maybe I should have accepted her offer, as I should have refused a week later to walk any further, just sat myself down on the Cape Cod sand until they found me. Instead I walked, trying in vain to look for my Ella's aging mother. Then, too, losing sight of Ella as she headed across the sand dunes. I walked. As I had on that Southern California beach with my shattered brother-in-law, through those Southern California malls with my ever-eager sister.

Maybe it was vanity that got in the way of thinking sensibly about my health. Six months pregnant and I never felt more beautiful, more "in shape," the round in my belly making me feel more woman, more lush, more fine and female. I walked and walked to keep that healthy rounding shape. I told myself that soon I will return home, stick my feet up on a lawn chair, and do nothing all San Francisco summer long but devote myself full-time to the task of growing larger with life. I had scheduled my work accordingly, canceled all travel by the seventh month (as recommended by my nurse), but the seventh month never came.

Beyond these ruminations of guilt and blame, I feel something deeper. I see pregnant women into their seventh and eighth and ninth month and envy them. I measure the shape of their belly against what I remember of my own. Did I get that far with my baby? How big was I? I don't experience this in a covetous way. I only long to recuperate those last three months of communion, getting big and fat and full of Rafa.

Sometimes I just chalk it up to one phrase: He was in a hurry to get here. I daily witness that quality in Rafaelito, always ahead of himself, always frustrated that his body hasn't quite caught up to where his spirit wants to take him.

I take hold of my breast, slide my fingers down to the nipple, squeeze the tip between my thumb and forefinger. This is how to get the milk going. To my surprise, a thick, rich yellow liquid spills out. I try the other side. Same thing. Although I go through this ritual every few months or so, checking to see if I can still make milk, this time—after days and days of writing, days and days of remembering those last weeks of pregnancy—the liquid is as thick as the day I gave birth. I think, *I could start all over again.*

I do miss it, at times, that intimacy with Rafael, remembering those tiny fingers greedily clamoring for my breast in the dark, finding it and latching on. His mouth, a kiss that lasted. At those moments, I felt I could recover a bit of the loss for both of us, our sudden separation from each other. And possibly that, too, is what this writing serves: to recover the loss by reliving those moments of first motherhood.

I stop here, put down my pen, cross to my son sleeping face down on the bed. I take him into my arms and marvel at his good health, his sturdy "thunder thighs," and the rich copper-rose color of his face.

I just feel damn grateful, as I am for Ella, remembering her Amazon strength, her Irish outrage, her basic loyalty during the hardest year of my life. She senses a change in me in recent months,

I know, a deepening toward her. "It's hormones, baby," I want to tell her. The proof is in that liquid life spilling out of my breasts.

Mid-July/Cape Cod

One year later, and Rafael has returned to this house, full bloom in my arms. We have settled into our stay here at the Cape with an open ease, and I feel myself very present with Ella, awed by her beauty. We touch each other. Often. There is a newness to the feeling, although it is always difficult mustering (not the word), conjuring (not the word), gettin' some full sex here. The house is quite small, and for what might sound like a fancy address, it's basically a working-class home where thin walls harbor few secrets.

It is very early morning, and the choice is between sleep and awakening to find these few moments alone to read and write. Rafael sleeps balled up into the corner of the port-a-crib, Ella lies belly-up, her hands cradling her pelvis that had her up earlier with menstrual cramps. In the next room, Ella's mother lies in a diagonal fetal position across her bed. Through the always-open crack of her door, I can see the well-shaped aging feet resting one upon the other. She's had another sleepless night, I ascertain from the reading glasses and curled paperback abandoned on the kitchen table, the open pack of solitaire cards next to them. I wonder how her mood will be today. All is dependent on the quality of her night's rest. When her body turns enemy—refusing sleep, spasming senselessly, stiffening in every joint—she becomes distant, preoccupied. But last night all those pains had vanished and she was pure delight. She, Ella, and I sat together well past midnight, drinking margaritas and telling stories. She was in her old best form, a spirited hard-hittin' talker...like her daughter.

The house rattles. Ella's mom must be up. I am beginning to recognize the sounds of her movements. During the first two nights here, the small staggered steps confused me. I thought them Rafael's, and I would

awaken with a start. Ella doesn't awaken, accustomed to the move-
ments of her mother, who cripples steadily. "Cripple." I cringe at the
harshness of the word. But what language is there to describe that
physical betrayal by the body in old age? Hers, more marked because
of the Parkinson's, yet I observe it in my own parents, less dramati-
cally, but nonetheless sudden. Always too sudden. Always sooner than
you expected. My mother turns eighty in November. Ten good years
maybe, I think. Then I think I'm being naively optimistic."

(And selfish). I witness my friends and their friends die overnight in their thirties and forties. I mourn la muerte de las madres
de mis hermanitas when they are still daughters in need of mothers. I remember my comadres who have always gone without. Without mothers, mothers themselves. And I realize the blessings of
longevity and good health in my familia. Still, I want to ask, "How
must it feel, Mamá, to live so close to death?" I don't dare ask.

Paul Monette's lover of ten years is dying. The book open on my lap, I
nod off to sleep. I dream I am dying of AIDS. We are all dying.

Provincetown

We spend the night at an inn. At 5:50 A.M. I give the baby a bottle and
struggle to get him to sleep again. An hour later I am wide awake and
he is warming my spot in the bed next to Ella, sound asleep. I grab my
journal and hit the streets. I love the opening up of a day, sitting on a
park bench in front of the P-town city hall. Twenty minutes ago, be-
fore I found this cup of coffee, the only noticeable activity was the
middle-aged joggers, the recycling truck, and the shopkeepers sweep-
ing up the brick sidewalks in front of their stores after a night's queer
frolicking.

It is a comfort, even as white as P-town is, to walk the streets here
unafraid with the baby on my back and Ella in hand. It is a comfort

after the queer wasteland of the rest of the Cape. P-town is a gay resort, although in the ten years or more since my last visit, it is glaringly evident that this place has suffered the loss of thousands of gay men. I can't really imagine the number who have visited here, now gone. AIDS virtually decimated Fire Island. They say the Provincetown Chamber of Commerce is beginning to worry cuz the dykes aren't nearly enough—in numbers or money—to sustain this resort town. So P-town is being pumped to the hets as a great place to bring the kids. And they do show up, little nuke families of 2.5 children, with daddy, always a hopelessly closeted queen, in the lead. By 9:00 P.M., however, they've all disappeared to their hotel cable tv's, and P-town once again plays gracious hostess to its ever-faithful queer clientele.

I could stay here forever in this fashion—reading, writing. Since I left San Francisco at the end of June, I have gone through such a range of emotions. One is the admission that I miss my morning writing time. Mornings were always my most creative hours, rolling out of a dream onto a page. A few days ago on the beach, I had been trying to finish the same page of Monette's memoir for fifteen minutes but kept getting interrupted by Rafa's insistent whine. I give up. I stuff Rafaelito into the carrying pack and onto my shoulders, announcing that "I have no internal life," and storm down the beach. High drama. I leave Ella with that comment, wanting to hurt her with it a little. I wanted to blame someone.

Ella complains of how slowly I move lately. It took me all morning to pack up the kid and me yesterday leaving for Provincetown. But I can't move any more quickly than that. Slowing down, I feel a deep weariness come to the surface of my bones, my skin. It is a residual exhaustion, the culmination of a full year and a half of endless work and worry: becoming pregnant, carrying Rafa for twenty-eight weeks, the three and one-half months Rafael spent in the ICN, the first year of his life adjusting to being here, our adjusting to him. The sleepless nights, the colds, the bowel problems, the writing deadlines in the midst of babycare, the relationship struggles because of babycare.

These days I am aware of a nameless ache inside of me. A longing for contemplation, reflection. Solitude sets in. I respond to it only in long walks along the beach, Rafaelito on my back. His excited kicks dig into my hips until he is lulled by the rhythmic rocking of my slow stride along the shore. The kicks subside, he sleeps. And I move into a kind of walking meditation.

The water here reflects the color of what I have only seen in the Mexican Caribbean. But this is not a Mexican sea; it is New England. In the distance I see Ella emerge from it, emerald sea-green. This is her color. The green of her eyes, her nature. This is her home, her immigrant land. I consider the two land masses of our origins—Northeast and Southwest—and wonder how she and I ever found each other, starting from such opposite ends of the continent.

Ella and I drift a distance from each other. There is a thin, sure cord between us. We keep the other afloat in a sea of an unspoken silence, so many dreams private and singularly sown. Do we drift apart? Her mother pulling her to the land of her childhood, and mine...?

Still, as the sun begins to disappear into the horizon, I think I could grow to love this place, begin to attach the smells and the texture and the wet weight of the night air to a sustained feeling, a memory, and make this strange land of occupying gringos something of my own. I watch my son take his own small-fisted hold of it.

Soon, should we continue to return each year, he will begin to remember Nana's home. Remember the nightly walk to the neighborhood pond. Remember the four ducks in perfect symmetrical harmony swimming in the pool of a full moon's reflection.

"Mira la luna," I say, days ago, pointing to the moon's uncompromised fullness. Will he remember "luna"? She, too, seems a kind of stranger here, a bit foreign in this land of summer storms and fierce bright winters. She is a Mexican moon.

And I dream of a desert
in which to bury us all
one day.
Mother, lover, child.
All.

2. A Child's Mark

The second year of our life together

I remember in the haze of a prolonged and private illness, an acute exhaustion, a longing for respite, finding none.

I feel I haven't really slept since the baby was born. How afraid I am...it feels so profound...to lay my head upon the pillow, that I may not rise up again.

I want to escape into a very deep sleep. All is my baby these days, and there is nothing left over for me.

What is this relentless exhaustion? The sudden rise in my body temperature, these cold sweats? I call and cancel all speaking engagements. I feel foolish, how little I know myself. How deep my weariness runs—quick bandaid fixes are not sufficient. How do I make a living? How do I give my child, my partner, the love they need? I worry about my "irregular" lifestyle—not my lesbianism, but my art—how it makes me travel, work nights, depend on the generosity of family and friends for childcare. I plot it all out compulsively weeks in advance. It is never enough.

I feel I have been asleep for days, endless days. I attribute it to jet lag, but I am returned home a week from the East and I am still sleepwalking.

I am some place not here.

I spy Rafael's smiles, his open-heartedness, his full presence that mirrors my own absence. I feel guilty I am missing Rafa, always missing him when my heart is pulled elsewhere inside myself. His wakefulness shames me, in comparison. I fear my obsessions. I fear anything that draws me away from this growing up of my child, but when I do not attend to my heart, I sleep anyway. Wordlessly.

I see an anger developing in Rafaelito. He threw a tantrum this morning, not knowing if he wanted his shoes on or off. I watch him in this stage of life before words, before I realize that exactly what he needs is to sleep like me. He, too, is exhausted, fighting cold after cold, ear infection after ear infection. I worry about all these health problems. Worry we're getting these viruses now from places where the environment has been ravaged and the earth's venganza returns to us the size of microbes. Is this paranoia or common sense?

Rafael awakens mid-sleep and utters a pained cry. I pat him softly and he drifts off again. Is it just that he needs to know we are there, or does he remember awakening at 3:00 A.M. under the hot glare of hospital lamps, no mama in sight, a sharp pain piercing his gut? I wonder where in his small body he has put all that suffering, what traces of it will reside in him as a grown man. An old man.

Santa Monica

This Southern California beachside hotel offers some respite with its trestles of bougainvillea, its terra cotta-tiled patio, its suggestion of a Mexican paradise. I sleep endlessly (Rafa staying with my mother). I cannot get enough sleep to restore those places in me virtually drained of all vitality.

I am sitting by the hotel pool with Ella. The world is brighter today, although the sea-sky threatens to break into thick rain, although my heart feels thick with breaking. Ella dreams of a Hollywood lifestyle. I've got no dreams except the lingering memory of the one I had this morning.

In my dream, the hotel's Mexican gardener wants to know why the gringos bring so much water with them. He means the rains, but I explain their fear of drinking Mexican water. (I am thirsty, too, all night sleeping with my mouth open and a stuffed nose.) I dream birds who look identical to babies but are really flying monsters. They have an insatiable hunger. Is it all me—this thirst? This hunger? This monstrosity?

I feel the monster coming out of midnight Mass.

It is Easter Sunday. I am kneeling in the yellowing wooden pew of my childhood church. Mass is being celebrated in honor of the parish's new converts. My father is one of them, draped in the same confirmation gowns I wore at twelve. My Tío Bobby, as his "sponsor," stands behind him on the altar steps. I watch the back of my father's balding head, that pink spot amid the last few feathers of a silver crown. Somehow in it I sense my father's vulnerability. He is receiving God. I know this is what he is thinking. After nearly five decades of living amongst us Mexican Catholics, my father has become one of "us." But I know I am no longer one of "them."

A two-and-a-half-hour service, and I am left spent and resentful. An empty ritual. I do not say this for the others, for my father's newfound faith. I say it for myself and my son, until he can speak for himself. My Catholicism—its Mexican symbols, its indianism—is such a private prayer that it no longer even resembles the religion. I am a heretic, not because I am faithless but because I am a believer—of something else, not here.

What to teach Rafael? I know this much: the small spirit-place we occupy in the universe. The common soul. A lighted candle that can ignite the fire of hope, of faith, of shared prayer. Shared prayers that stop wars, cure wounds, mend hearts.

I believe this. I believe in an emptiness that can be filled with selflessness. I don't know how to arrive there. I don't know how to even find the path, but I will clamber toward it in the dark with my son by my hand. Until it is time to let go.

One year ago, I relinquished Rafaelito to his godparents at the baptismal fount of a humble East Los Angeles church. It is the church of the poor, and the presiding priest, a pastor of the poor. Still, when they return Rafaelito's newly christened self back into my arms, I feel I have betrayed him. I hold him tight against the breast of an unanswered prayer. I want to protect my son from deceit, from the failure of male gods and god-fearing males.

That night I dream murder, mayhem. I dream them against us.

Ella and I are going to slaughter. Along with dozens of women, we are to be executed en masse. There is a war going on and we have been taken captive. I realize I have been separated from Rafael, that he is alone in our apartment. I shout this out loud, hoping I will be spared to save my son. This is exactly what happens. A guard hears me and takes pity. He leaves a gate open through which I can escape. Of course, Ella (not being the "real" mother) is not allowed out, but to my great relief I learn that she, too, is released later.

I am afraid of the power of men and their gods over our lives. I fear this even as I write it. I protect/protest my life by separateness, by secrets, by never speaking aloud my own spiritual creed. I have constructed my daily life, to the degree to which I am able, outside the prison of patriarchy. This is not a rhetorical statement. This is the fact of my existence and the home-world in which I will raise my son. I am not fooled. They are not fooled. Even motherhood does not make me loyal to them.

Here in Southern California where it snows in the foothills during Easter week, birds of paradise grow to the size of monsters and their urgent beak-mouths gape open to the heavens. Are they hungry too? For what? The foreboding rains?

It is springtime and Easter and I try to convince my aching bones, my ailing heart, that the season will bring a change, a resurrection of hope, a return of faith.

It does not.

This is the second year of our life together.

I dream I have lost everything. All material possessions. I have lost my writing on the most profound of levels. No trace of it is left. It is as if all that I had previously written has disappeared.

I am hysterical. Like a child, I wail on the floor. I throw a fit. Ella is a man in the dream. S/he is having a business meeting with an artist. S/he is no comfort, s/he cannot console me. I go to my room, continue my ranting and raving. Myrtha enters. I tell her what has happened. I remember someone saying, "Moving out of the darkness into the light." She tells me this is all a blessing. To begin again as an artist, completely clean, from scratch, not burdened by the past of your previous writings.

I awaken this morning with a small stone inside my breast.

I feel Ella's name etched into the stone. Is it her, or only a nameless uncertainty in me? We go about our lives in separate orbits. I want the distance in a way. I must confess that in some of my imaginings of the future, I do not see her clearly formed there. I only know my son's constant presence, and maybe that speaks to something of this "lover" quality to my feelings with him. He just won't up and leave. Not yet.

Maybe "lover" has been replaced with "mother" these days, but it does not satiate. At times I miss la pasión, fear how remote it has become between Ella and me. Worse, fear it no longer matters to me, which I know is a lie, a camouflage waiting in the bushes to jump out and fall on some other woman's bones.

It's so hard with Ella. Her energy dominates my life. I blame her, unfairly, for the voice inside me I cannot hear. The writer's voice. My home has become my fiercely guarded sanctuary. I want to control it all: the quiet, the comings and goings of familia and friends, the order of my day and night with Rafaelito.

I feel a lot of water under the bridge, a lot of plain not-saying. I fear we may have taken this relationship (as partners/lovers) its full course. I don't trust my fears, but cannot rid myself of this sense of hopelessness. Are we slowly splitting off from each other? Is that the weight I feel inside my chest?

Kids separate you. Kids bring you together. They literally separate you in the bed, worming their animal-selves between two grown women's breasts and hips and entangled thighs. They sneak into the bed at three o'clock in the morning, when they know you are too tired to resist. And our middle-aged mothers' bodies contort to make room for them, waking hours later with stiff necks and out-of-joint hips. Another night without sex. Nights become weeks. Weeks become months. Until someone finally wrestles the other into the bed, for the sheer lesbian pride of it (neither of us willing to live a sexless life).

I remember that lesbian pride as we walked the streets of Provincetown with Rafaelito and Ella's mother, months ago, Nana's pale freckled hand tucked into the crook of Ella's arm. Ella, ever observant, tells me on the sly how "different" the dynamic is when I am pushing Rafaelito in the stroller and she is guiding her mother down the crowded main drag.

"Now that's interesting." She is adamant. "The butch mom and her kid, the femme strolling with her mother. That's a compelling couple." When we change positions, Ella is struck by the sudden absence of lingering glances from the other dykes along the crowded main drag.

"You walking with my mom, me pushing the stroller. The butch daughter, the femme mom with her child. Nah, that's predictable." I love her for this. Her continued delight at our lesbianism, still savoring the "style" we generate from each other after so many years together. It is not superficial. It is hard won through great opposition. It is renewal, that mutual commitment to the rebellion of female loving, even into our forties. We are not domesticated loving. Keep your marriages, I say to myself. I want the freedom of this unpredictable desire. I want to stay awake.

But there are days when I have fallen back asleep.

Ella comes in for a kiss and I turn my mouth to her cheek instead. She feels spurned. I explain it as my fear of giving her a cold. We know this is an excuse. We know this is not what I fear. We fight.

We fight in the morning. Then again in the evening. We fight because there is not enough room—amid travel schedules and work weeks and childcare and groceries and doctors and writing and not-writing and laundry and dishes and grant deadlines and meetings—to need each other.

We fight about work: housework, art work, political work. We fight about what is and is not our work.

"Practice what you preach," Ella blazes me with her fiery tongue. Yet I remain removed. I do not wholly take risks. I am afraid of selling my soul to the devil. The devil of commerce, the devil of my "commitment to community."

Ambition is the enemy of art, I want to tell her. I don't tell her I want to write like vocation, like spirit-saints at the foot of the bed. This is the only religion I want to enter, the cloister of my own writer's cell. I am afraid of compromising the privacy I've learned to defend so passionately against all odds, against all causes. To write.

We fight, Rafael our silent witness.

He sits in his highchair in front of a bowl of bananas. He watches our faces. He doesn't yet fully understand all the words, but tone and gesture tell him we are angry. Today I do not have enough time to be both mom and playwright. Then suddenly, mid-argument, Rafael points his finger at each of us and says, "No."

We stop fighting. Kids bring you together...

She is remembering hope.

The other night, Ella cried over the loss of socialism, the loss of "even one country, the small size of El Salvador," she said, as an emblem of resistance. She is remembering a revolution...lost. She is remembering lost romance. I cry with her, but I am not she. I do not see myself in Tina Modotti who threw away her camera for communism. I will never throw my "camera" away for any cause.

Still, Ella's "cause" compels me. And there are full days when I think only of giving her all the support she needs, not abandoning her. Trying to have the long view, trying to love someone bent on doing something, finally, for a change.

Ella asked me to find my own heart. She says she cannot stay with me any longer if I do not examine my real feelings and be willing to change. I am not open to Ella. I don't know what to say to her. I don't know how to come back. I am always protecting myself from Ella. What do I fear she will take from me?

I remember the first time with Ella, she walking up the hill to greet me. I remember her smiling in a field of light. This was the first sense I had of her, a brightness that enlivens, her generosity of spirit.

I am awed at times by that sudden beauty between us—what is conjured spontaneously, sin trabajo. But it has felt so long since that meetings of souls. We are best just hanging out, driving in the car, taking a little trip with Rafa. We are family then. We are best just the three of us, no world pressing down upon us. Is it the world that divides?

Sueño

Estoy con mi carnalita, una morena. Lésbica. There are two paths in
the dream. One high, one low, leading to the same destination. The
lower path runs along the shoreline. We choose this one. Follow it. The
vista is breathtaking. A turquoise water lapping against a bleached
Mexican desert sand. There are deer in the distance. They, too, are
turquoise—the Indian color of precious stone.

I am at a pivotal point on the path, that place where desert
storms make signs impossible to read. I squint, curl my toes into
the pebbly earth, dig in. I ain't budging 'til I know, I insist. Then
worry that I'll be found buried here, waiting to see the road dream-
clear.

The Road Dream-Clear

The sun has dropped to the level where the peaks of the Cape Cod
sand dunes rise to catch it and the shadows of all us bathing-suited
bodies loom large and perfectly delineated in the wet-ribbed sand.
Rafa is caught by the movement of the shapes. Still, I don't know if he
quite understands the relationship between the motion of my now
wildly waving hands and the dancing forms shadowed in the sand.
What he does discover and thoroughly entertains him are "footprints."
It is the first time I've used the word with him, I realize, although not
the first footprints we've made together. But these footprints are unde-
niable. At first, he studies the deep outline shaped by my step, then
jumps into it, his small step disappearing into my own. Only when I
catch on that this is what fascinates him so do I give it name and
more shape in his child's imagination. He continues on down the
beach, jumping with both feet now, shouting "footprints, footprints." I
see his wonder, and then the sudden pause of disappointment when
he finds sand that doesn't adhere so readily. "Too wet," I tell him in

Spanish. "Too hard, mijo," I explain in other places as we make our way down the shore to meet the quickly receding laps of pond-like waves.

Then the words come to me. "Fall asleep to wake up"—that sudden forgetting of self in the act of wholly living a moment. It is a Zen notion to be sure, but seldom so completely realized except through the gift of one's teacher-son. Seeing through his fresh and innocent vision, Rafaelito is my lens, the prescription for these aging and forgetful eyes. All is about an acute awareness, waking up to those moments in our lives when there exists nothing else but this simple word, "footprint," for our original child's mark upon the planet: I am here, sweet earth.

There is no yesterday, tomorrow, or last year. Yet, there is all of it—the brittle bones of our ancianos, the heavy hearts of lovers, whole years lost to sleep—which dissipates in the unself-conscious and thoroughly present naming of the imprint of a child's foot in the sand.

3. Blood Matters

In the third year of our life together

Ella moves out of our home. Not out of my arms or Rafa's reach, but into a peace of mind, a piece of home she can call her own.

The growing presence of Rafael in our lives filled up that space that was once reserved for our selves together and apart: our selves as lovers, our selves as creators, our selves that once had the luxury of picking up the slack when somebody else was slacking. My own lack of generosity toward Ella—the absurd tightening I'd feel in my gut at the sound of late-night "politica" (strategies debated over telephone wires) or the sight of a neglected dirty dish—finally forced Ella out of the house.

It was not an easy move to make, nor to counter the voices inside our heads arguing that this would mean the end of our family together. It has not. Maybe this is the gift of middle-aged loving, a more compassionate understanding of our own needs, our own natural limits. Easier to change a living arrangement than a cellular one.

What the move apart did do was lay bare all that has sustained and separated Ella and me beyond the domestic. Living together, our quarrels were not profound, and only on occasion, profane. The deeper questions remain and lie buried beneath the stones we carry inside our hearts. The commitment we continue to make to each other is to slowly unearth them, one by one, as we can. It is a "till life do we part" promise, and life sometimes does part us.

As does death.

November 1996/San Francisco

I stand in the kitchen with my sister. I dip my hands into the dishwater. I scrub, rinse, stack. She cries about the death of...what?

Twenty years of a loveless marriage? More? Who can count when we stopped counting, stopped caring, only to stop mid-step, mid-life, and calculate with a vengeance how many good years left, good looks left, good waistlines, jawlines, bustlines. Men and time a suddenly shrinking commodity in my sister's newly singular mind, while four hundred miles south of here my uncle at seventy-six assumes the ninety-six-year-old dying body of my grandmother, his mother. How long ago was that death? I have to count to know. (She would've been one hundred and ten years old in 1998.)

I say to Jo Ann, "Life is about loss. It's all loss." She suffers over this, emerging enflamed from the fire of first real love at forty-five. We taste that life fleetingly, slipping through the sieve of our ever-hungry hands.

Southern California

My Uncle Bobby's hands are elegant in their sudden skeleton-shaped delicacy. His skin, a smooth glove of dried parchment. I could write the story of our lives there—in the steady caress of his hand, his softening face, so female. His female tears, his fears. He tells me, "I need the strength to face this. I am afraid I don't have the strength."

He is pure grace, my tío, always a class act, even in rumpled flannels. Even at death's door. Since the news of his impending death I have been seeing that door in my day- and night-dreams like a silent movie running behind my eyeballs. I am reminded of how simple and childlike are the images we conjure of death: an ordinary wooden door opening to a black starless sky; a spaceman without his spacesuit—without the body inside the suit—floating.

We are all dumb animals. We know death is coming, the circle drawing tighter and tighter around us until we are pressed into the core-heart of the moment of that knowledge. And yet, we continue to lie to ourselves that we are not my dying uncle, my mother in a handful of years, my baby's almost-lost life. Why do we think it won't happen to us? The length of our lives is a kind of cruel joke whether you're eight or eighty watching the silver brilliance of death's blade enter. It splits open the sternum of our denial into two perfectly unsymmetrical halves, the heart half-falling out of its home, still pulsing and animal alive. *I am not ready to stop. Not yet,* it laments.

We each find out we are to die within a fragment of a second in the cosmic hour. Still the giants give us time to prepare to fly, the body ages dramatically. We become old men overnight. We are as close to divine as we can get.

I see God in my tío because he is closer to death than anyone I have ever known by heart, except for my son. I take my son to visit my dying uncle, to offer my uncle comfort and cariño; to bring my son closer to his history and his future. I will tell him years from now when it matters, "Yes, you met him. You knew him. You climbed upon the thin bones of his thighs and kissed him full-mouthed on the cheek. He cried."

The next day my uncle is angry he cannot flick the ashes of the cigarette he is dying to have in the last days of lung cancer. He is too weak to make the long arm's journey from parched lip to doily-covered nightstand where the ashtray waits to receive him like a ghost. All the furniture talking now, making up stories about the lives they've seen pass through these doors.

She, the wife, the one not looking at God yet, only at an old man dying (the wife couldn't fall asleep unless she had his arm for a pillow under her head), can't sleep now waiting for God to take away her armrest. He's angry and she's sleepless and there's no rest for the wicked, we all fear. But there is no wickedness here. Only two human hearts dissolving.

I am trying to write about the impossible, the ordinary beginning of one life and the passing of another. Watching a life enter and another exit within the same brief moment of my family's history.

I dream my mother, Rafaelito, and I are standing on an outdoor elevated porch when an earthquake hits. I instantly grab my mother with one hand, my son with the other. At first I enjoy the temblor's intensity and assure them both, "Just hold on. It'll pass." We ride the wave of the quake with tentative pleasure until suddenly it unexpectedly intensifies. The porch begins to collapse beneath us, the house next door caves in. I feel I am losing hold of them both. As the quake rocks and rolls us I soon realize we may not survive, and I try with all the strength in my being to bring my son into me, to protect him from death. He is slipping beyond my reach. My mother has left my consciousness. I awaken.

Primordial struggle. Trying to hold onto she who precedes me, he who follows. Forces beyond my control.

My uncle is dying. Is this the first time in my life that a pain has left me empty? No broken heart/no welling tear ducts/no bruise or blood? I had always named this hollow feeling woman-hungry. But I am not hungry. I am not lonely. I am empty, but not free.

It is a crime to remember death in every waking moment of one's life. It is unnatural, unearthly. My son's dance—stockinged feet kicking up the bedroom carpet, three-year-old karate-chopping hands flying—becomes a death dance because I think of nothing else but to love and lose, to lose whom you love, to lose that you love.

My parents have visited my dying uncle for what they know will be the last time. They walk out of the small ground-floor apartment into the thin chill of a Southern Californian December. They cross the lawn to their car, where my father unlocks and holds open the door for my mother. She gets in. He goes around to the driver's side and gets in. They sit side by side in their sweaters in the front seat of the Buick and cry. Nobody ashamed of the tears, nobody faking it. Together, they have known my uncle at least as long as they have known each other, fifty years next year. They cry together...like old lovers.

With the death of my querido tío I find myself having to explain my sudden absence of spirit, my mourning over a "mere" uncle. "He was like a father to me," I say, perfunctorily, hating the lie in the expression. My tío was not my father. I have a father. He was my uncle, my mother's little brother whom she raised like a son in a family that does not separate cousin from sister from brother from blood. He was my uncle who fathered my younger cousin Cynthia, whose loss I suffer like a sister. He was my uncle. It matters.

My tío's death has ruptured that intimate circle of familia that is the last real generation of the Mexican-American Moraga clan: those World War II veterans and their worker-wives having kids in the '40s and '50s, kids they hoped would be more than the bartenders, electronics assemblers, upholsterers, truck drivers, waitresses, housewives, railroad and factory workers they were. Some of us are more (economically and educationally), some of us aren't; but none of us are as much family as they. And as my uncle's generation goes, the family goes with it in that profoundly Mexican sense.

We waited too long,

When we arrive, Rafaelito's abuelo is already in a coma. We waited because Pablo, so new to fatherhood, didn't know if it was his place to ask. I didn't know if it was our place to go. Both Pablo and I trying to figure out what blood and bones had to do with this business of making queer familia. But we're Mexicans. Blood matters. So, at the last

minute, I take Rafaelito to Los Angeles to visit "Tata," his dying pater-
nal grandfather. Rafaelito is not allowed to enter any further than the
door of the ICU room. His tender age makes him too vulnerable to the
deadly infection Tata carries in his lungs. I take hold of Tata's sleep-
ing hand and sense in it an electric current, charged and living, pass-
ing between this dying man and his grandson whom Pablo holds in
his arms. It is a mutual connection. There is no explaining this. My
son and his tata have never met.

A full year after his father's death, Pablo tells me, "I know my
father is gone. I don't feel his presence, but he speaks to the kids."
He means his nieces, especially Fiona, the youngest, who casually
refers to her tata as if he still occupied a place at the dinner table,
on the couch, in the sun on the front porch steps.

"He speaks to Rafael, too," I tell Pablo.

And as my altar clutters with the images of those who have passed on,
my child learns the sacredness of candlelight and murmured prayer.
Do I hear their voices, the voices of the dead? I don't know. At times I
pray quietly, with no resonance other than the vibration of my own
silent wording within the temporal geography of my body. But Rafael
is listening and answers to the calling of his tata's and tío's name,
"Amen."

Día de Lupe

My uncle died on the feast day of the Immaculate Conception on
December 8, 1996. Four days later, on December 12, he is buried on el
Día de la Virgen de Guadalupe. And in the span of those two feast
days—the first to honor the North American Virgin Mother, the second
to honor the Mexican—the story of my uncle and all my family is told:
U.S.-born and Mexican-blood.

At my uncle's funeral, my father, a man unaccustomed to speaking in public, mounts the pulpit and declares aloud to the congregation, "He was my brother." My father is Anglo. But Mexican is the only way we know how to make familia.

And I dream of a desert to bury us all one day.

Epilogue: The Messenger of Death

When you told me about the funeral, it amazed me how we/they acknowledge you as the family scribe, the "seer." How rare it is that a family can see and appreciate that across differences and generations.... It is because your work, your life honors them.

Letter from Ella

A Sunday morning

Ella and I converse and caress in bed, arms and legs draped around each other. She and I have grown closer since her move, the desire returning. I feel her softening and I, too, soften to the touch. She has lost a lot of weight (from nerves and overwork mostly), but her body has a suppleness to it, a vulnerability that invites me. There are times I feel her skin moving slowly into aging (that quality of softening). At other times, the softness feels like a kind of rejuvenation and a laying down of arms.

I admit I miss the "daily" with Ella at times, as does Rafa, I know. Still, for us, less has proved best. "I can't try and follow the rules no more," I had told Ella. "No more this is what 'a couple' is supposed to look like. We are what a couple looks like." We are what a family looks like.

Suddenly, the drumroll of two small bare feet can be heard from the next bedroom. They speed across the living room hardwood floor and then across the kitchen into our bedroom where they lift off the ground, transporting their pajama-clad, Pooh bear-towing owner onto our bed. Rafa muscles his way in between Ella and me, throwing his arms around my neck. "My mami," he asserts. Playing along, Ella retorts, "My girlfriend." Rafa ups the ante, "*My* girlfriend." And the "custody battle" over mami ensues. Ella's and my eyes meet. We don't speak to it, but the joy we draw from this love triangle is measureless.

I watch Rafael, at three years old, take on the characteristics of Ella's animated humor, her flare for the dramatic and simple righteousness. There is no accounting for love. No accounting for what finally makes a family, except love. I remain awed by this mystery of how love and blood and home and history and desire coalesce and collide to construct a child's sense of self and family. I know blood quantum does not determine parenthood any more than it determines culture. Still, I know blood matters. It just does not matter more than love.

An hour later, and Rafael and Ella have fallen back asleep. I rise, Ella stirs in bed. Her presence is well-placed and rides deep in me, lingering as I slip out of the covers, slip into sweat pants, slipper my way into my study.

From its window, I write with the view of the overgrown clover-filled garden: the giant cedar split vertically at its peak after a harsh winter's storm, the bald spot of exposed fence where once a tree sprawled diseased and beautiful. It was uprooted and carried away in a dumpster. To my left, the skeletal frame of a fruit tree, never bearing fruit. To my right an avocado, also childless.

I suspect my description of all this, including the fallen telephone line tangled in the barbed wire of the driveway gate, calls forth little beauty in the imagination. But all is lovely to me and changing. It has just begun to rain, ever so delicately, so lightly it can't be heard. I can only see it silver against the deep forest-green backdrop of the cedar. Rafa's toys abandoned in the winter cold are now being engulfed by the growing clover. They are bright spots of primary plastic colors amid the complexity of nature's hues.

I love this place. This spot of chaos and growth amid industrial San Francisco. My home. Maybe I write this way because I sense I am leaving this place of rose-colored geranium and blossoming lavender sage. Are those irises breaking through the mound of clover and succulent? It feels good to write like this, my woman and child sleeping. It feels good to write "my woman and child" without ambivalence.

The flame from my altar candle dances in a double (vaguely triple) mirror reflection in the window. It is raining harder now and the flame insists. Changes.

The hardest loving is what is required of me as a mother: the letting go as the feelings deepen between my son and me. How can I describe the lesson—that each day there is a birth and a dying of this time in our lives together, that with a child one sees it so clearly because the changes are physically and dramatically manifested.

Rafael Angel is a messenger of death, not in the negative sense of the word, but in that he brings the news of the cruel and sudden miracle of the cycle of our lives. I could write he is a messenger of life, but I know it is truer to acknowledge that my sometimes quiet sadness at the deepest moments of joy with my child has to do with this complete knowledge of impermanence. In the face of that knowledge, I visit my aging parents, bring my woman coffee in bed, and stroke the silk of my son's hair.

This, too, will pass.

19 abril
Día del indio, 1997

Sources

Dorothy Allison. *Two or Three Things I Know for Sure*. New York: Dutton, 1995.

Tede Matthews. "Angel Wings" (unpublished poem).

Paul Monette. *Borrowed Time*. New York: Harcourt Brace Jovanovich, 1988.

Michel de Montaigne. *The Essays of Michel de Montaigne*, translated and edited by M. A. Screech. London: Allen Lane, 1991.

Toni Morrison. *Jazz,* New York: Alfred P. Knopf, 1992.

Leslie Marmon Silko. *Almanac of the Dead,* New York: Simon & Schuster, 1991.